Learning Unity 2D Game Development by Example

Create your own line of successful 2D games with Unity!

Venita Pereira

PUBLISHING

BIRMINGHAM - MUMBAI

Learning Unity 2D Game Development by Example

First published: August 2014

Production reference: 1180814

Published by Packt Publishing Ltd.
Livery Place
35 Livery Street
Birmingham B3 2PB, UK.

ISBN 978-1-78355-904-6

www.packtpub.com

Cover image by Kerrie Woollhouse (kerriewoollhouse@hotmail.co.uk)

Credits

Author
Venita Pereira

Reviewers
Clifford Champion

Adam Single

Kerrie Woollhouse

Commissioning Editor
Luke Presland

Acquisition Editors
James Jones

Rebecca Pedley

Content Development Editor
Poonam Jain

Technical Editor
Edwin Moses

Copy Editors
Sarang Chari

Gladson Monteiro

Project Coordinator
Mary Alex

Proofreaders
Simran Bhogal

Maria Gould

Ameesha Green

Paul Hindle

Indexers
Hemangini Bari

Mariammal Chettiyar

Tejal Soni

Graphics
Ronak Dhruv

Production Coordinators
Kyle Albuquerque

Conidon Miranda

Cover Work
Conidon Miranda

About the Author

Venita Pereira is hugely passionate about games having grown up on games since she was 7 years old. She is a games connoisseur who enjoys all types of games—no game is too big or too small—and a technology geek who enjoys all things technical. She studied at the University of Pretoria and holds a Bachelor's degree in Information Science, specializing in Multimedia, and over 7 years' experience working in the gaming industry. She has worked on all platforms, including console, PC, and mobile, on a wide range of genres.

Venita Pereira has worked for some of the biggest AAA companies, namely, Climax, Team17 Digital Ltd., Ideaworks3D, Jagex, SEGA, and Full Fat and for some of the biggest publishers: Activision, Square Enix, EA, and Hasbro.

Her softography includes Sonic Dash, Sonic Jump, Stellar Dawn MMO, Transformers: Dark of the Moon, King of the Course Golf, Lara Croft and the Guardian of Light, Alien Breed Trilogy, Leisure Suit Larry: Box Office Bust, and Elveon.

With a big special thanks, I would like to dedicate this book to Kerrie Woollhouse.

I would like to thank my mom, dad, and sister Michelle for all their love and support. Thanks to the Packt Publishing staff for their assistance through the process and the technical reviewers for their feedback. I would also like to thank God, my family, and friends.

And finally to the little girl Isabelle Woollhouse with a big heart, for believing in me!

About the Reviewers

Clifford Champion has a broad background in software engineering, with years of experience spanning 3D games, Internet applications, and AI. He holds degrees in Mathematics and Computer Science from UCLA and UCSD respectively. In the past, he worked at real-time physics company Havok, and interactive media and design company PlainJoe Studios. Currently, he is a member of the software team at zSpace (http://zspace.com/), helping create interactive 3D displays and software for classrooms, industry, and entertainment.

Clifford can be found on Twitter at @duckmaestro and welcomes discussion on any topic.

Adam Single is a husband, father, professional developer, indie developer, lover of music, and a gamer. He's the coder for 7Bit Hero; a programmer on the tech team at Real Serious Games in Brisbane, Australia; co-founder, programmer, and co-designer at Sly Budgie; and co-organizer of the Game Technology Brisbane Meetup.

Since entering the professional game development industry in 2011, Adam has worked on numerous mobile games, including the Android hit Photon and a preinstall game for specific Disney Japan handsets. He's been the programmer on a team that created a huge, interactive display at Queensland University of Technology's amazing multi-touch screen installation The Cube as a part of Australia's first Digital Writing Residency. He has even worked on a team at Real Serious Games creating large-scale, interactive simulations for the mining and construction industries. All of this has been done using the Unity game engine.

Adam has a passion for the unique and engaging possibilities inherent in modern technology. When he's not working on exciting new game mechanics for Sly Budgie, he's experimenting with homemade VR using mobile phone technology and pushing the exciting ideas behind 7Bit Hero's live music/multiplayer game interaction down whichever fascinating path it may lead.

Kerrie Woollhouse is a very creative and artistic individual with 7 years of experience in game development, web development, art, and photography. She continues to follow her passions with high ambitions.

I would like to say a special thank you to the greatest inspirations in my life, my amazing mum and dad, two beautiful sisters, and three wonderful brothers. I would also like to thank Packt Publishing and most of all a big thank you to Venita Pereira.

www.PacktPub.com

Support files, eBooks, discount offers, and more

You might want to visit www.PacktPub.com for support files and downloads related to your book.

Did you know that Packt offers eBook versions of every book published, with PDF and ePub files available? You can upgrade to the eBook version at www.PacktPub.com and as a print book customer, you are entitled to a discount on the eBook copy. Get in touch with us at service@packtpub.com for more details.

At www.PacktPub.com, you can also read a collection of free technical articles, sign up for a range of free newsletters and receive exclusive discounts and offers on Packt books and eBooks.

http://PacktLib.PacktPub.com

Do you need instant solutions to your IT questions? PacktLib is Packt's online digital book library. Here, you can access, read and search across Packt's entire library of books.

Why subscribe?

- Fully searchable across every book published by Packt
- Copy and paste, print and bookmark content
- On demand and accessible via web browser

Free access for Packt account holders

If you have an account with Packt at www.PacktPub.com, you can use this to access PacktLib today and view nine entirely free books. Simply use your login credentials for immediate access.

Table of Contents

Preface   **1**

Chapter 1: Getting to Know Unity   **7**
Overview   **7**
Game development's background   **7**
Introducing Unity   **8**
Setting up Unity   **8**
Creating a new 2D project   **9**
Unity Editor interface   **11**
  Toolbar   12
  Scene View   14
  Game View   14
Project Browser   **15**
  Creating assets   15
  Searching assets   16
  Setting favorites   16
    The Unity Asset Store   17
    Importing assets   17
  Hierarchy   18
    Parenting   18
    Creating GameObjects   19
  The Inspector   20
    Adding components   21
Extra Views   **22**
  Console   22
    Animation   23
    Sprite Editor   23
    Animator   24
    Profiler   24
Summary   **25**

Chapter 2: Setting the Scene — 27

Overview — 27
What is a background? — 27
Two methods to set a background — 28
  Setting a background using a static image — 28
    Importing our asset — 28
  Sprite settings within the Inspector — 30
    Texture Type — 30
    Sprite Mode — 31
    Packing Tag — 31
    Pixels to Units — 31
    Pivot — 32
    Filter Mode — 32
    Platform Settings — 33
    Applying our settings — 34
  Assigning our asset to a GameObject — 34
    The toolbar method — 35
    The quick alternative method — 38
  GameObject Inspector settings — 39
    Position background — 39
    Color background — 39
    Layer background — 39
Setting a background using a tileset — 40
  Seamless textures — 41
  Corner pieces — 41
  The grid settings — 41
  Creating a prefab — 41
The resulting environment — 41
  Camera settings — 42
  Setting the foreground — 43
Summary — 44

Chapter 3: Add Some Character — 45

Overview — 45
What is a sprite? — 46
Creating a sprite — 46
  Image editing software — 46
  Sprite sheet — 47
  Raster versus vector — 48
  File formats — 49
Importing a sprite — 50
Slicing sprite sheets — 51
  Sprite Editor — 52

Manual slicing	53
Adding and removing a selection area	54
Toolbar controls	55
Automatic slicing	**56**
Slicing type – automatic	56
Slicing type – grid	57
Texture atlasing	**61**
What is a texture atlas?	61
Sprite packer	62
Adding our character	**63**
Sprite Renderer	**66**
Animating a sprite	**69**
Animation Editor	**70**
Dopesheet 2D animation	**70**
Animator	**72**
Summary	**73**
Chapter 4: Code Control	**75**
Overview	**75**
Why do we need code?	**76**
Programming languages	76
Levels of programming languages	76
Machine language	76
Assembly language	77
High-level languages	77
Scripting languages	78
UnityScript versus C# versus Boo	79
Code fundamentals	**81**
Data types	81
Operators	82
Functions	83
Conditional statements	86
If...else	86
Using comments	87
Classes	87
Private versus public	88
Importing external libraries	88
Code editor	89
Hello world	**90**
Controlling the character	**92**
Destroying the enemy	**94**
Coroutines	**99**
Namespaces	**100**

Unity Scripting Reference	**100**
Summary	**102**
Chapter 5: What's Your Input?	**103**
Overview	**103**
Input versus output	**103**
Input in games	104
Output in games	105
Input types	**106**
Output types	**107**
Visual output	108
Audio	108
Controller vibration	109
Unity Input Manager	**110**
Detecting input	**111**
Buttons	**112**
OnGui	112
GUILayout.Button	112
Game controls	**114**
Raycasting	114
Summary	**118**
Chapter 6: Game #1 – Roguelike	**119**
Overview	**119**
What is Roguelike?	**120**
Adding a background	**122**
Animating the hero	**123**
The Walking Down animation	124
The Walking Left animation	126
The Walking Right animation	127
The Walking Up animation	127
Movement controls	**128**
Movement Controls Animator	128
Movement controls script	130
Randomly spawning enemies	**136**
Animating the enemy	**138**
Enemy movement	**138**
Shooting projectiles	**141**
Detecting collisions	**143**
Permadeath	**144**
End game result	**145**
Summary	**145**

Chapter 7: Game #2 – Classic Arcade   147
Overview   147
Sponge antics   147
  Our main character – Spongy   148
  The bathroom   148
  Adding Spongy   149
  Moving left and right   150
  Spawning grime   153
  Spawning acid   156
Game conditions   158
  Lives   158
  Score   159
  Time   159
Adding an HUD   159
Font style   160
Resource management   161
The completed game   163
Summary   164

Chapter 8: Game #3 – Endless Runner   165
Overview   165
Infinite   166
An agile ninja   166
The ninja character   167
  Running   167
  Jump and Slide   168
  Add animator parameters   170
  Animator states and transitions   170
  Movement controls   172
Randomly repeating obstacles   175
Survival   178
Parallax scrolling   178
Add pizzazz with particle effects   180
Displaying the timer   181
The result   183
How to expand the game?   183
Summary   184

Chapter 9: Game #4 – Physics Fun   185
Overview   185
The basics of physics   186
  Physics found in the real world   186

Physics 2D	**187**
What is Box2D?	**189**
Steps to create bodies	**191**
Let's simulate the world	**194**
The environment	194
Creating the scene	194
Creating the background	194
The foreground	195
Adding the props	196
Shooting the cannonballs	197
Creating the cannonballs	202
The final result	**203**
How do we extend it?	**205**
Summary	**205**
Chapter 10: You Are Ready!	**207**
Overview	**207**
Audio	**208**
Music	208
Sound effects	208
Saving and loading	**209**
Creating a trigger	**209**
Cameras	**210**
Multiplayer	**210**
Putting it all together	**211**
The first scene	212
The galaxy	212
Platforms	213
Triggers	213
The lava	214
UFO beam	215
Adding audio	**215**
The camera	**216**
Saving and loading	**217**
Space Buddy the alien	**217**
Space Buddy script	227
Positioning	228
The second scene	**228**
The final result	229
Deployment	**232**
Your journey ahead	**233**

A plethora of resources   **234**
    Online resources   234
    Offline events   235
    Free resources   235
    Hosting games   236
Social media   **236**
Summary   **236**
Index   **237**

Preface

Many of us enjoy games, are creative and imaginative, and want to be able to create our very own games — now more than ever before. Whether it is simply for fun, out of pure passion, or as a career, the game development industry is currently one of the biggest, most rewarding, and most lucrative industries.

For this very reason, there are many analogies of game development being compared to or synonymous with the gold rush. We all have a vision, but a lot of the time, we either do not know how to go about it, or we go about it in the wrong way.

The aim of this book is to help beginners start on the right path by explaining game development as a whole and then breaking it down into its simplest components, making it easy to digest. Those already proficient in Unity will be able to learn the new 2D features quickly and easily.

When creating games, there are always new things to learn and discover, and no single book can teach everything because every one of us will want to create a huge variety of game mechanics and scenarios. However, the book covers all the essential foundations through a variety of genres so that by the end of it we will be able to create any game that we so desire.

What this book covers

Chapter 1, *Getting to Know Unity*, takes a look at how to work with Unity's new 2D workflow by creating a 2D scene using the new project option available. We will then step through the Views that make up the Unity Editor interface.

Chapter 2, *Setting the Scene*, shows us how to work with the new 2D camera to set up the scene with different types of backgrounds, either static or dynamically using a tileset.

Chapter 3, Add Some Character, provides an overview on how to add a character to the game by making use of the new sprite toolset. We will also learn about 2D animation by creating a simple idle animation for the character using the new dopesheet feature.

Chapter 4, Code Control, goes through the core concepts of programming by creating basic code in UnityScript that takes us from printing output to controlling a character and destroying an enemy.

Chapter 5, What's Your Input?, teaches us all about the various input types and states. We will then go on to learn how to create buttons and the game controls by using code snippets for input detection.

Chapter 6, Game #1 – Roguelike, shows us how to create our first basic 2D game in Unity with UnityScript. This game will include movement, collisions, triggers, states, projectiles, boundaries, and randomly spawning entities.

Chapter 7, Game #2 – Classic Arcade, informs us about game conditions and how to display them on the screen by implementing a HUD with all the UI elements in a classic arcade game.

Chapter 8, Game #3 – Endless Runner, provides an insight into the new 2D parallax scrolling in Unity and how to use it to create our own side-scrolling endless runner, polished up with particle effects.

Chapter 9, Game #4 – Physics Fun, takes a look at the new Box2D physics in Unity and how to use this to create a physics game similar to *Angry Birds* that simulates real-world physics.

Chapter 10, You Are Ready!, prepares us for our onward journey with audio, feedback, and deploying our game. We will use everything that we have learned throughout the book to create a game similar to Doodle Jump. We will then be guided on our onward journey in 2D game development with a selection of useful resources.

What you need for this book

This book can be read without any additional resources; however, we recommend access to some physical lab resources to install Unity on and at least a trial version of Unity. The first chapter walks us through downloading and installing Unity.

A reasonable lab setup can be one on a single physical host with at least a dual or quad core processor and 8 GB (preferably) of RAM.

Who this book is for

If you are interested in creating your very own 2D games, even if you are a beginner who is completely new to Unity or someone who has used Unity before and would like to learn about the new 2D features of Unity, this book is for you.

Conventions

In this book, you will find a number of styles of text that distinguish between different kinds of information. Here are some examples of these styles, and an explanation of their meaning.

Code words in text, database table names, folder names, filenames, file extensions, pathnames, dummy URLs, user input, and Twitter handles are shown as follows: "The Debug.Log() function is very useful for debugging/testing our games."

A block of code is set as follows:

```
function Update ()
{
renderer.enabled = false;
}
```

When we wish to draw your attention to a particular part of a code block, the relevant lines or items are set in bold:

```
acidInstance = Instantiate(acid, Vector3(Random.Range(-8, 8),7,0),
  Quaternion.Euler(new Vector3(0,0,0)));
acidInstance.name = "Acid(Clone)";
acidInstance.velocity = new Vector2(0, speed);
```

New terms and **important words** are shown in bold. Words that you see on the screen, in menus or dialog boxes for example, appear in the text like this: "Go to **File | New Project**."

Warnings or important notes appear in a box like this. Comments that appear with the code are also included in such a box.

Tips and tricks appear like this.

Reader feedback

Feedback from our readers is always welcome. Let us know what you think about this book—what you liked or may have disliked. Reader feedback is important for us to develop titles that you really get the most out of.

To send us general feedback, simply send an e-mail to feedback@packtpub.com, and mention the book title via the subject of your message.

If there is a topic that you have expertise in and you are interested in either writing or contributing to a book, see our author guide on www.packtpub.com/authors.

Customer support

Now that you are the proud owner of a Packt book, we have a number of things to help you to get the most from your purchase.

Downloading the example code and colored images

You can download the example code and colored images for all Packt books you have purchased from your account at http://www.packtpub.com. If you purchased this book elsewhere, you can visit http://www.packtpub.com/support and register to have the files e-mailed directly to you.

Errata

Although we have taken every care to ensure the accuracy of our content, mistakes do happen. If you find a mistake in one of our books—maybe a mistake in the text or the code—we would be grateful if you would report this to us. By doing so, you can save other readers from frustration and help us improve subsequent versions of this book. If you find any errata, please report them by visiting http://www.packtpub.com/submit-errata, selecting your book, clicking on the **errata submission form** link, and entering the details of your errata. Once your errata are verified, your submission will be accepted and the errata will be uploaded on our website, or added to any list of existing errata, under the Errata section of that title. Any existing errata can be viewed by selecting your title from http://www.packtpub.com/support.

Piracy

Piracy of copyright material on the Internet is an ongoing problem across all media. At Packt, we take the protection of our copyright and licenses very seriously. If you come across any illegal copies of our works, in any form, on the Internet, please provide us with the location address or website name immediately so that we can pursue a remedy.

Please contact us at `copyright@packtpub.com` with a link to the suspected pirated material.

We appreciate your help in protecting our authors, and our ability to bring you valuable content.

Questions

You can contact us at `questions@packtpub.com` if you are having a problem with any aspect of the book, and we will do our best to address it.

1
Getting to Know Unity

"Microsoft, which is now the biggest independent software company in the world, was founded in 1975 by just two men. It goes to show that great oaks from little acorns grow."

– Cambridge Idioms Dictionary, 2nd ed.
Cambridge University Press, 2006

Overview

In this chapter, we will briefly go through the following:

- Game development's background
- An introduction to the Unity engine
- How to work with Unity's new 2D workflow by creating a 2D scene using the new project option available
- The Views that make up the Unity Editor interface

Game development's background

In the past, the business of creating games was either for a lone programmer in their garage or an established game development company backed up by a publisher. When game development was still in its early beginnings, the former was more common; however, as the technology behind game creation improved, it became more difficult and expensive for an individual to create even a simple game from scratch. In order to do so, you needed to create a game engine—the core of a game that runs all the different technological components needed to support a game.

Game engines were built from scratch for a specific game genre, and they took a long amount of time, effort, and resources. It was a complex task that usually required advanced knowledge of math, science, and programming. Although, since the fundamentals of game development come down to the same principles, it is more efficient to build upon the foundations instead of reinventing the wheel.

Therefore, game engines and game-authoring tools became readily available and more general purpose for the mainstream public who were interested in pursuing game development. Instead of worrying about the functionality, we can now concentrate more on the gameplay.

Introducing Unity

Unity is a popular game engine because of its accessibility, simplicity, and vast amount of features. It has a big developer community and a free indie version available. Many successful games that have massive marketing budgets and are developed for major platforms, from PCs and consoles to mobiles (also known as AAA games in games industry lingo), have been made using Unity. More importantly, it is very popular in the indie community. Many highly popular indie 2D games were made using Unity. A major feature of Unity is being able to create your game once and then deploy it on every major platform.

Unity originated as a 3D engine, and as such has mostly been used to create 3D games in the market. However, as there is such a high demand for 2D creation tools with many 2D games being released, particularly with the popularity of app development, the developers of Unity have just recently released tools specific to 2D creation in Version 4.3.

Setting up Unity

We are going to set up our Unity workspace in this section. To download and install Unity, execute the following steps:

1. Go to `http://unity3d.com/unity/download`.

2. If we are installing Unity for the very first time, then we will need to sign up for a Unity account first through `https://store.unity3d.com/account/users/new`.

3. Click on **Looking for an older version?** under the **Download Unity** button.

4. We need to ensure that we select and download Unity version 4.3.4 for our platform, whether it is a PC or Mac.

5. Follow the onscreen prompts during the installation.

6. Make sure not to uncheck the default components as we will need them when creating our games.

7. Once we have successfully installed Unity, we need to run the application. Run the `Unity.exe` application.

Creating a new 2D project

We will now create our first 2D project in Unity by executing the following steps:

1. Go to **File | New Project**.

   If this is the very first time that we have installed Unity, then we will not see the **File** menu option, but instead, we see the **Unity - Project Wizard** window.

2. The **Unity - Project Wizard** window is similar to the ones in previous versions with the exception of an added drop-down box that now allows 2D.

3. The **Create New Project** tab will be selected by default. If it is not already selected, then click on the tab to create a new project.

4. Select the location on your computer where you would like to save your new project files either by entering it directly in the **Project Location** textbox or finding it via the **Browse** button.

5. From the **Setup defaults for:** drop-down box, select **2D**. This will ensure that our project is set to 2D mode.

   The following screenshot shows what we will see on the screen:

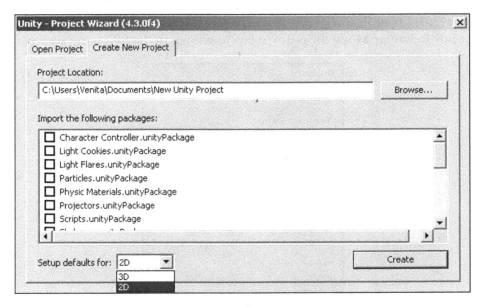

6. Now, we simply click on the **Create** button to create our new 2D project in Unity.

Once we have created our new 2D project, we can also toggle the view from 3D to 2D and vice versa. Whenever we wish to do so, we just click on **2D** in the Scene View control bar, as shown in the following screenshot:

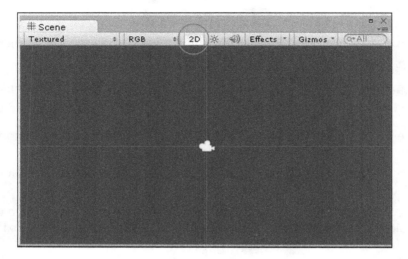

We can select 2D before we create our new 2D project or any time after we have created it by going to **Edit | Project Settings | Editor**.

This will open the **Editor Settings** toolbar within the **Inspector** tab, which by default is on the right side of the program. We can select the 2D mode by selecting **2D** within the **Default Behavior Mode** drop-down box as shown in the following screenshot:

Unity Editor interface

We are now going to familiarize ourselves with the **Unity Editor interface** so that we know our way around Unity.

The main editor window is made up of **Views**. Views are all the tabbed windows that you see, namely:

- **Toolbar**
- **Scene**
- **Game**
- **Project Browser**
- **Hierarchy**
- **Inspector**
- Other Views that are not shown by default

We can see the main editor with all of its Views, which were just mentioned, in the following screenshot:

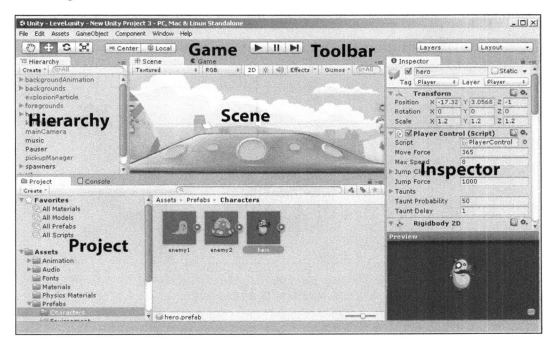

Toolbar

At the very top of the editor interface, we have all the controls.

The Transform tools are used with Scene View to drag the camera, move the position of objects, and rotate and scale objects in the scene respectively, as shown in the following screenshot:

When we add an object to our scene and select it, we can see arrows protruding along the *x* and *y* axes from our object. These arrows are called Transform Gizmos, and we use them to move, rotate, and size our objects.

Selecting each of the following Transform tools changes the gizmo (the bounding box on your selected object) in Scene View, as shown in the screenshot that follows the description of the tools:

- **Translate** (the shortcut key is *W*): This is used to move the selected object in our scene
- **Rotate** (the shortcut key is *E*): This is used to rotate our selected object
- **Scale** (the shortcut key is *R*): This is used to increase or decrease the size of our object

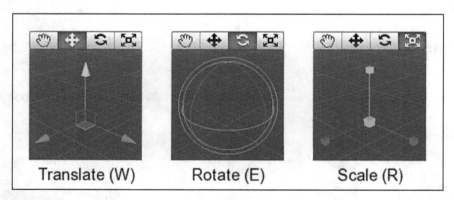

Transform Gizmos, viewed 26 June 2014, `http://docs.unity3d.com/412/Documentation/ Manual/PositioningGameObjects.html`

The screenshot is in 3D because even in 2D, we can still move objects along the *z* axis.

The Transform Gizmo toggles are used to toggle the position of the Transform Gizmos. **Center** will position them at the center of the object, whereas **Local** will position them relative to the object's rotation. The toggles are displayed in the following screenshot:

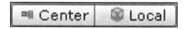

The following screenshot shows the control that is used with Game View to play, pause, and step through the game in the editor:

The **Layers** drop-down box is used with Scene View to choose which objects we want to see in the editor's Scene View according to the layer. It is useful when we are editing a complicated level or scene. We select it by clicking on the drop-down menu displayed in the following screenshot:

The **Layout** drop-down menu enables us to set up the positioning of the interface to our own liking. Depending on our screen's resolution and size, we may prefer one layout over another and should therefore try each one out by clicking on the drop-down menu shown in the following screenshot:

Scene View

Scene View is the area where we will interact with our GameObjects such as cameras, backgrounds, the player, enemies, and so on. It is within this view that we can position and transform our GameObjects.

The following screenshot displays our Scene View:

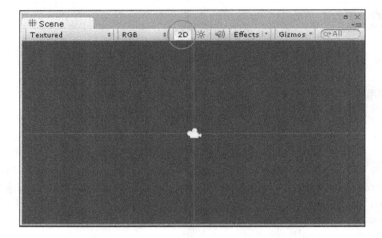

Game View

Game View displays the final published game rendered from the camera view. This is where we test out our game.

To achieve this, we simply press the play button and see our game as in the following screenshot, where an example game has been loaded:

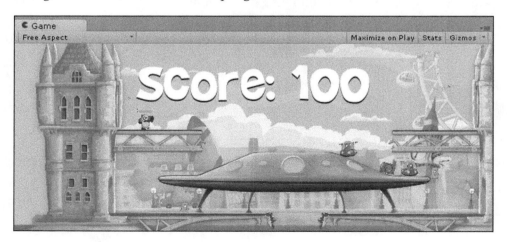

Project Browser

Assets are image files, audio files, programming scripts, and so on that make up the reusable mix-and-match pieces of our game.

Project Browser contains all the assets; it lists them in a project and allows us to view and organize them in folders, as shown in the following screenshot:

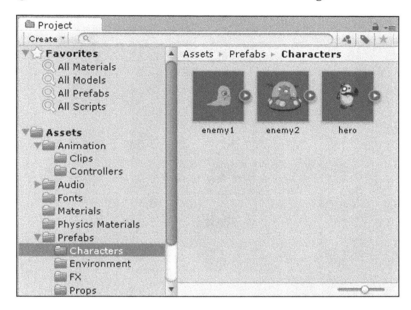

In the left panel are the folders that contain our assets in an ordered structure/hierarchy that we will create when creating our games.

Different assets in our project such as materials, animation, audio, and so on should be placed in their own folders, often in further subcategories for clarity.

On the right panel are the asset files from the selected folder, and they can be edited here.

Creating assets

When making a game, some assets will be created outside of Unity (such as in an image-editing or sound-recording program). Those assets will be imported into Unity to be used, while other assets can be created inside of Unity, such as cameras, game objects, scripts, and animations.

When we click on **Create**, at the top of the left panel, we are given a list of assets that we can create, as shown in the following screenshot:

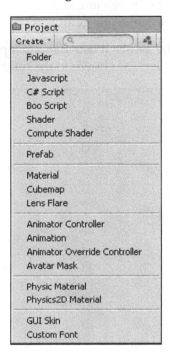

Searching assets

We can easily search for any asset from the Project Browser toolbar. This is done by either selecting the label button to search by its name or selecting the type button to search by its type. Depending on which button we select, we type either the asset's name or type in the search bar and then press *Enter* to search.

Setting favorites

Assets that are used often can be set as favorites by clicking on the star button. For quick and easy access, we can then search for or filter them under the **Favorites** drop-down menu in the left panel.

The Unity Asset Store

Asset Store is an online marketplace created by Unity for independent game developers to buy and sell reusable assets to make games, as shown in the following screenshot:

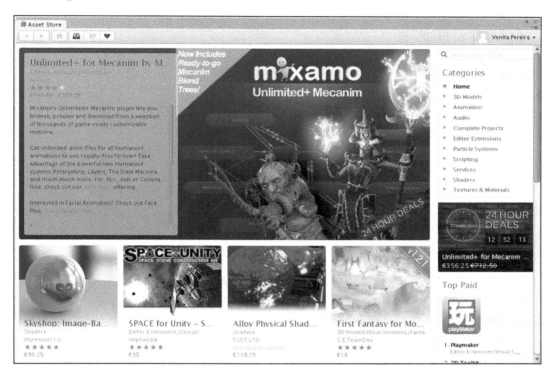

Any assets purchased or downloaded from Asset Store will be shown and can be accessed from Project Browser.

Importing assets

To load our assets from the Asset Store into the Project Browser, we need to click on the **Download** button on the chosen asset within Asset Store.

The **Importing package** pop-up box will appear within the Unity editor, allowing us to tick the assets we would like to import. Once we are done selecting, we simply click on the **Import** button to import the assets into our project.

Hierarchy

The **Hierarchy** tab lists all the GameObjects in the current scene. Scenes are made up of game objects, and game objects make use of assets. We can easily access any GameObject in the scene from the **Hierarchy** tab for quick editing.

The following screenshot displays the Hierarchy view with the game objects in black and prefabs in blue:

Parenting

Parenting is a hierarchical concept that affects the visual pose of game objects in relation to another object's pose, for instance, the parent's pose. A child's translation, rotation, and scale will be relative to the parent. So, we only need to edit the parent's relative transform data and the children will inherit them. This is useful for animating multiple separate images by changing their position. For instance, if we have an arm and a hand image, then we make the arm the parent and the hand the child, once we do this, we only need to move the arm and the hand will move in relation to it.

Creating GameObjects

When we click on **Create**, we are given a list of preconfigured GameObjects that we can create, as shown in the following screenshot:

Although the list may appear daunting, we will not need to concern ourselves with many of these GameObjects as most of them are used for 3D games. The only GameObjects we will be using are the Particle System, Camera, GUI Text, and Sprites.

The Inspector

Game objects are the *living things* in our games, and the different components are what bring a game object to life in different ways. For example, the Audio Source component allows a game object to emit a sound, while a Script component allows a game object to behave intelligently or respond to user input.

When we click on a GameObject within our scene, the Inspector provides detailed information about that object. It displays all the components that have been added to the selected GameObject, such as animations, colliders, scripts, and so on, as well as all the attributes within the components. This allows us to directly modify its fields and their respective values from the Inspector.

> We can also change the values during runtime to test the effect in real time while running the game. However, this is only used to temporarily test the effect of the changes. Once we stop the game, the values will revert to their previous settings. Therefore, only the changes we make while not running the game are saved instantly.

We can reset any changes by right-clicking on the component and selecting **reset**.

By clicking on the red, green, and blue cubes in the top-left corner, we can set an icon to label our GameObject within Scene View, making it easier to find them.

Whenever we do not want a component active at any time, we can simply deselect the component by deselecting the box. We do this to temporarily turn it off without losing its settings, because had we deleted it, then we would have lost any changes made to the default settings.

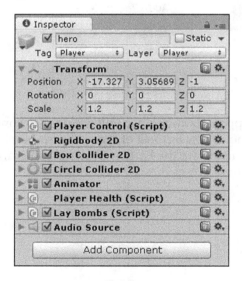

Adding components

To add a component to the selected GameObject, we click on the **Add Component** button. When we click on **Add Component**, we are given a list of components that we can create, as shown in the following screenshot:

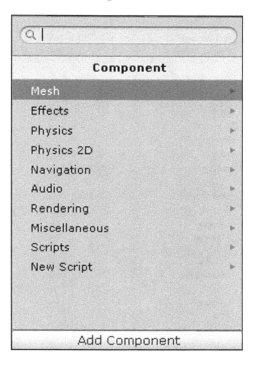

We can also remove a component by right-clicking on it within the Inspector and selecting **Remove Component**.

Extra Views

Other than the six main Views of the editor interface that are shown by default, there are extra Views that are also very useful. We can select them by clicking on the **Window** menu:

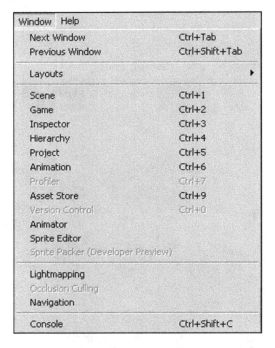

Console

The Console View is useful when you write code to output messages and to check for any problems with the code. Any warnings and errors in the code will be displayed here.

These messages only appear to us developers to test and debug our game and will not be shown in the final game to the players. The following screenshot displays the Console View:

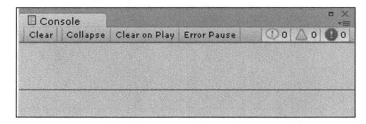

Animation

The Animation View is used to animate the GameObjects in our scene using an animation timeline with frames, as shown in the following screenshot:

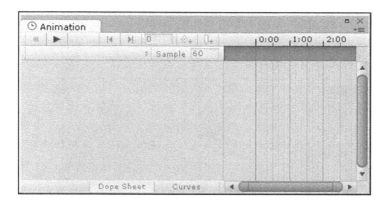

We will discuss this in great detail in the later chapters.

Sprite Editor

Sprite Editor enables us to separate merged images (known as a sprite sheet or The sprite atlas) from a single image (or sprite as it is often called in the world of 2D). It is useful, for example, for animations and when we want different parts of our character to move independently, as shown in the following screenshot:

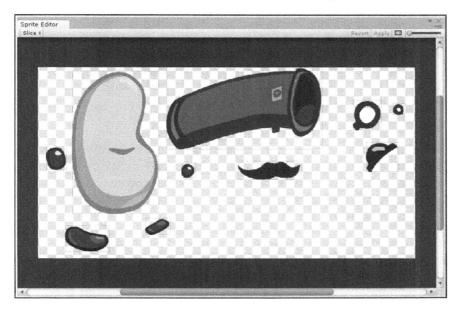

Animator

Animator controls the order of an animation. It provides an easy way to set up animations by visually representing the flow of the animation, such as the completion of a jump animation leading to a standing animation. It enables us to create animation states. We can then order the flow of animations and decide when one animation state transitions or blends into the next state, as shown in the following screenshot:

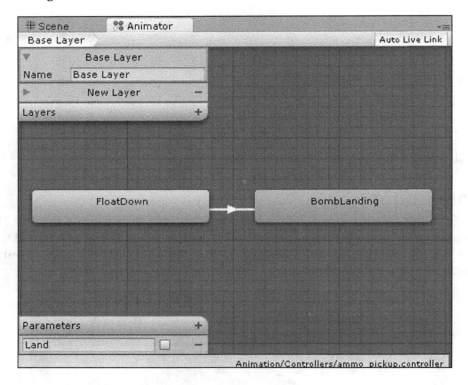

Profiler

Profiler (a feature that comes with the Pro version) is used to check on a game's performance (how fast it runs) and on what could be slowing it down with regards to memory usage, object count (total objects), draw calls, and so forth. Different things can slow down a game, such as too many sprites on the screen at the same time, very complex AI or scripts, and so on.

The standard benchmark for a game is to run at 60 FPS (frames per second). It is recommended that anything less than this should be optimized and improved. This ideal frame rate varies from genre to genre and platform to platform. For instance, an RPG game is generally acceptable at 30 FPS, whereas a racing game is best at 60 FPS.

The following is a screenshot of Profiler:

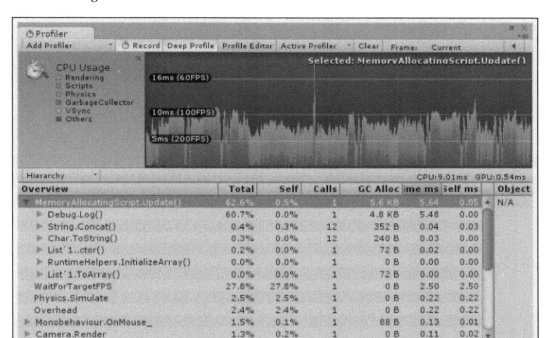

Unity Profiler, viewed 25 June 2014, `http://www.gamasutra.com/blogs/`
`WendelinReich/20131119/203842/C_Memory_Management_for_Unity_`
`Developers_part_2_of_3.php`

Summary

In this chapter, we went through the background of game development and were introduced to the game engine we will be using, namely Unity Engine.

We also learned how to work with Unity's new 2D workflow by creating a 2D scene using the new project option available and then stepped through the six main Editor Views that make up the Unity Editor interface. We also went through the additional Views that are available.

In the next chapter, we will look at setting up our own scene. We will set up all the elements that make up our environment, namely the camera and the background.

2
Setting the Scene

"In many 2D tile-based games, the background is very unobtrusive. It is typically a very large distance from the game plane, meaning that there is no ambiguity as to whether or not something is part of the background or the playground. All of this amounts to a very clear level."

– Chris McEntee, 2013

Overview

In this chapter, we will go through the following elements that will create our scene:

- What is a background?
- Two methods used to set a background:
    - ° Setting a background using a static image
    - ° Setting a background using a tileset
- The resulting environment

What is a background?

A background is the image or images that are furthest from view, usually behind the characters and objects in the game.

It adds a scene to our game, an environment that our game will take place in, to immerse the players in the game world.

Sometimes, a background can be static (non moving) and most of the time the player cannot interact with the background as it is more of a visual element to provide the setting, tone, and mood of the game.

The following image represents a background:

Two methods to set a background

We will learn how to set up our scene with a static background using two methods:

- Using a static image
- Using a tileset

Setting a background using a static image

When we want only a few images of different sizes to make up our background, we use static images.

Importing our asset

First, we will need to either create an image or select a pre existing image that we will be using as our background by finding its location on our PC, as shown in the following screenshot:

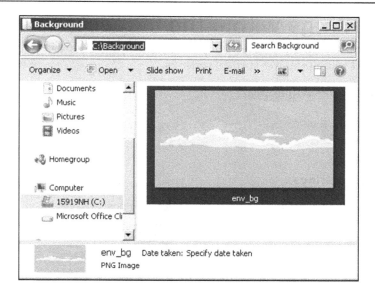

For clarity and organizational purposes, it is best to create a Sprites Folder within the Project Browser with a subfolder called Environment to store all the assets that we will use to create our game environment.

To create the subfolder, we right-click on the Assets folder in the left-hand side panel of the Project Browser and go to **Create | Folder**, or we can click on the **Create** button at the top of the left panel.

We then drag our image into the **Assets** section of the Environment subfolder within the Project Browser, which is shown in the following screenshot:

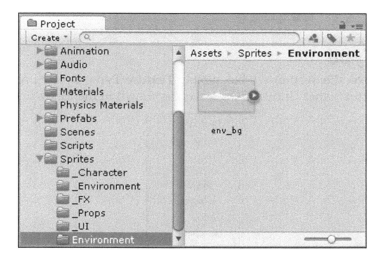

Sprite settings within the Inspector

When we select our imported asset from within the Project Browser, the Inspector will get updated to display the sprite's settings.

The following settings will appear:

- **Texture Type**
- **Sprite Mode**
- **Filter Mode**
- **Platform Settings**

These settings will appear as shown in the following screenshot:

Texture Type

When we click on the drop-down box next to **Texture Type**, we are presented with the types of textures that Unity makes use of, as shown in the following screenshot:

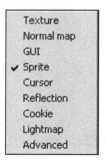

As we are working in 2D, we would like to use an image, and therefore, a sprite, as our background. Thus, we will select **Sprite** as our Texture Type. It is important to select the correct type as each type will update and display unique settings within the Inspector that are dependent on the Texture type.

Sprite Mode

For the Sprite Mode, we are presented with two options: **Single** and **Multiple**, as shown in the following screenshot:

We will choose **Single** as we want to create only one sprite that uses the whole image.

Packing Tag

We will leave the **Packing Tag** box blank because we do not need to concern ourselves with this setting. It is an advanced pro-only feature used for automatic sprite packing, otherwise known as **texture atlasing**.

Texture atlasing is used when separate sprites/textures are packed together to form one sprite/texture to improve frame rate (performance) when drawing many sprites per frame.

The following screenshot displays the **Packing Tag** box:

Pixels to Units

The **Pixels to Units** property is used when we import an image and it either appears much smaller or much larger than intended. If the image appears much larger, we set this value lower; otherwise, we set this value higher. By default, the value is set to 100, as shown in the following screenshot:

Pivot

The Pivot property sets the point on the image from where you would like to move it. All the values are preset locations with the exception of **Custom**, which allows us to choose any point on the image by dragging the anchor point to our desired location within the Scene View. We can select whichever we prefer; however, to be able to center the image easily and quickly, we will set the **Pivot** property to **Center**, as shown in the following screenshot:

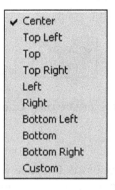

Filter Mode

The Filter Mode setting determines how the texture used for the sprite gets filtered. Have a look at the following list of settings:

- **Point**: This is the cheapest (relative to the cost on computer performance) and best for performance, but is used for smaller images that are further away as the image will look blocky if you view it up close.

- **Bilinear**: This is more expensive than Point; however, it smoothens the image so that it is not blocky up close.

- **Trilinear**: This is similar to Bilinear in that the image is no longer blocky up close; however, it is the most expensive on performance as it also smoothly transitions **mipmaps**. Mipmaps are used to improve performance when many textures are used. When a texture is far from view, then it will use a low resolution and swap to textures of higher resolution the closer it comes into view.

Bilinear is selected by default. As we are not making use of mipmaps, we need to only select **Bilinear** as displayed in the following screenshot:

Platform Settings

There is the option to set specific settings for each platform (the Web, mobile, and PC) that we would like to target for our game by selecting the relevant icon as well as ticking the **Override** option. These settings will then override the default settings, which are the **Max Size** and **Format** settings, that we are now going to set within the **Default** tab, as shown in the following screenshot:

We will leave it on **Default** so that it will apply the same settings for all platforms.

Max size

The **Max Size** setting sets the maximum size when importing the texture for our background sprite. Different platforms will require different resolutions. We will use a high resolution of 1024, as shown in the following screenshot:

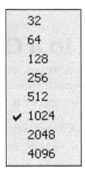

Format

There are several options available that will represent the image internally:

- **Compressed**: This is the default and is the most commonly used option, being the smallest in size
- **16 bits**: This option is for images that are larger in size and higher in quality than **Compressed**, but lower in quality when compared to **Truecolor**
- **Truecolor**: This is the highest quality option, but the largest in size

As we want our game to run on all platforms, we will select the **Compressed** format as shown in the following screenshot:

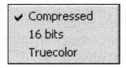

If we were targeting only high-performance platforms, then we could select the higher quality formats.

Applying our settings

When we are done and happy with our settings, we need to make sure to click on **Apply** so that our settings are saved and take effect. This completes the import process, and we are now ready to use the sprite in our scene.

Should we wish to go back to the default settings, we can click on **Revert** instead.

Both buttons are displayed in the following screenshot:

Assigning our asset to a GameObject

Now that we have imported the asset that we would like to use as our background and have set all the settings that we would like to use for it, we can assign the asset into a GameObject so that we can make use of it within the game.

Once an asset is assigned into a GameObject, we can then view and manipulate it within the Inspector and Scene View as well as view the end result within the Game View.

To convert our asset into a GameObject, there are two ways: the toolbar method and the quick alternative method.

The toolbar method

The first way is to select the **GameObject** drop-down box from the top toolbar by going to **GameObject | Create Other | Sprite**.

We will be presented with what is shown in the following screenshot:

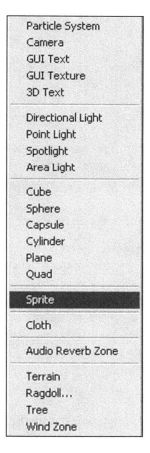

We click on **Sprite** as we will be working with sprites to create our background.

The GameObject we have just created will be empty within the Scene View, as shown in the following screenshot:

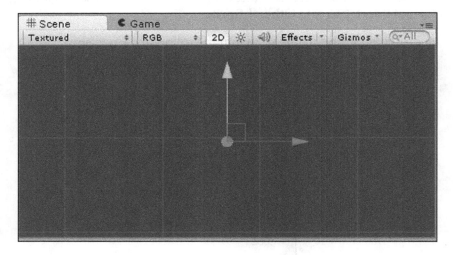

You can name the GameObject and move it; however, it has no visual appearance yet.

We need to assign the sprite asset we created to the GameObject by clicking on the circle next to **Sprite**, as shown in the following screenshot:

Once we have clicked on the circle, we will get the **Select Sprite** box.

Under the **Assets** tab, we can find and select our asset, as shown in the following screenshot:

The quick alternative method

Another alternative to assigning the sprite is by dragging the sprite from the Project Browser and dropping it into the **Sprite** box just before the circle, as shown in the following screenshot:

 The quickest and simplest way to create a Sprite GameObject is to simply drag the asset sprite from the Project Browser into the Scene View.

All methods should result in what's shown in the following screenshot:

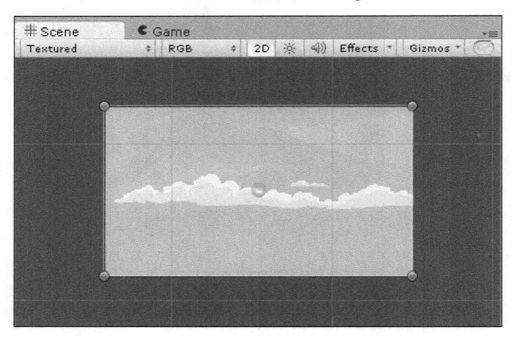

As you can see, our centered pivot anchor point that we set during the asset import settings stage is now displayed, and should we change the pivot then the anchor point will update within the Scene View.

We can now move the GameObject and its image in the Scene View from its center.

GameObject Inspector settings

The settings that we set for the GameObject within the Inspector will take effect within the Scene View.

Position background

To position the background so that it fits perfectly within the 2D Camera View, we go to **Inspector | Transform | Position** and set the following values:

- **X**: 0
- **Y**: 0
- **Z**: 0

This sets the image's central anchor point to the origin of the Scene View's coordinates.

If the image is smaller than the Camera View, then we can scale the image so that it is large enough to fill the entire view.

The size of the Camera View will depend on the platform that we have chosen to build and run our game on in addition to our camera scale settings. The platform can be changed by going to **File | Build Settings...**.

Color background

We also have the option to color the background or use advanced artistic effects by choosing shaders to use on the material of our image. Unity comes with a basic set of shaders.

Layer background

We can leave our background on the default layer as it needs to be beneath all the images that we will create on layers above it. This layer is known as the Sorting layer.

Setting a background using a tileset

Tilesets are sets of tiled images that are used to create the scene, as shown in the following image:

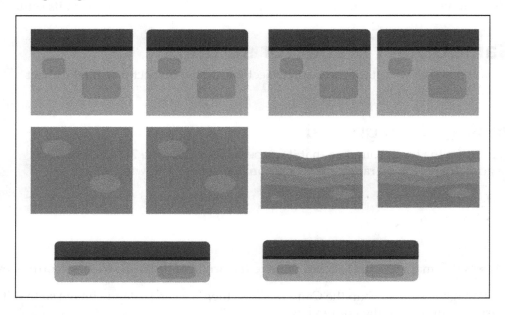

Some games, especially platform games, puzzle games, and sandbox games use tilesets to create their backgrounds.

Using a tileset makes it easier to create and edit those types of games because the tiles get reused to make the scene in different variations.

Tilesets require the following:

- Seamless textures
- Corner pieces
- Grid
- Prefab (not required, but it helps make the creation process much more efficient)

Seamless textures

The images that will be used as tiles within a tileset need to be seamless and of equal or matching size. This is so when you duplicate them and then arrange them next to each other or above one another, they will then blend nicely together to create the bigger picture.

Corner pieces

Depending on the type of game we would like to create, we will more than likely require corner pieces when creating a tileset to round off the edges of a section of the background and break up the repetition. We need to ensure that the corner pieces can be rotated and fit together from all angles.

The grid settings

To easily and accurately place our tiles, we need to work with a grid that the tiles snap onto so that the tiles fit and match together properly.

To edit the Unity grid settings as per our own liking, we go to **Edit | Snap Settings...**. We then hold *Crtl* + drag to place and snap our tiles onto the grid.

Creating a prefab

A prefab is a reusable GameObject. When we add a prefab to the scene, then an instance of that GameObject is created. This means that if we make any changes to the prefab, then all the instances will automatically change, saving us a lot of time. Therefore, when dealing with a tileset, it is a good idea to create a prefab of each unique tile by dragging the GameObject in the **Hierarchy** tab into the **Project** Browser. The name of your GameObject in the **Hierarchy** tab will turn blue to signify that it is now a Prefab.

The resulting environment

With the new 2D features of Unity, the 2D camera is already set. This makes it easier to set up our scene as we need only worry about positioning the background and foreground elements and layering them.

Camera settings

We will go through the camera settings to understand them. When we click on the **Main Camera** option in our scene, we get the following settings within the **Inspector** tab as shown in the following screenshot:

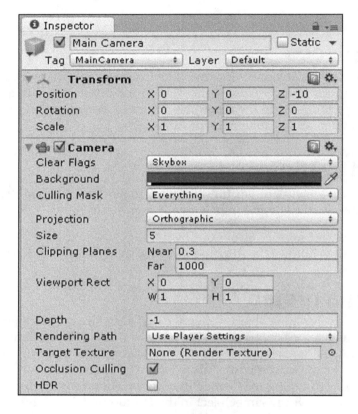

The following are the parameters of the **Main Camera** option:

- **Clear Flags**: This sets which parts of the screen are to be cleared.
- **Background**: This selects which color to display behind all the objects in our scene if we have not added a skybox, background, or image that takes up the whole screen.
- **Culling Mask**: This selects which layers are to be rendered by the camera.

- **Projection**: We select **Perspective** if we want to work in 3D and **Orthographic** to set our camera mode to 2D.

- **Size**: This is the size of the camera in Orthographic (2D) mode.

- **Clipping Planes**: This sets the distances from the camera that we would like to begin and end rendering.

- **Viewport Rect**: This consists of the camera's x and y coordinates followed by its width and height.

- **Depth**: This is the draw order of the camera. Cameras with bigger values will be drawn above cameras with smaller values.

- **Rendering Path**: This defines advanced rendering methods used by the camera.

- **Target Texture**: This references the output of the Camera View to a Render Texture (pro-only feature).

- **Occlusion Cullling**: This disables rendering of objects not seen by the camera

- **HDR**: This sets **High Dynamic Range** rendering. (An advanced rendering technique — visual effect that reproduces a more dynamic range of luminosity).

Setting the foreground

For the foreground, we go through the same steps as we did for the background, the only difference being that we will need to set the foreground images to layers above the background. As we set the background to 0 earlier, for the foreground we set **Order in Layer** to 1 so that it is above the background, as shown in the following screenshot:

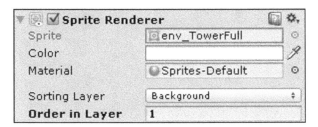

The following screenshot shows an example of a complete scene, with the foreground layers above the background layer:

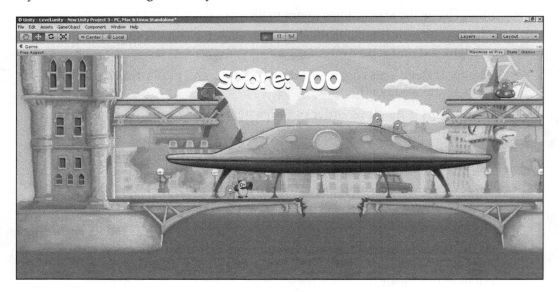

Summary

In this chapter, we learned the purpose of a background in a game and the two methods to set a background. Finally, we learned how all the elements make up the resulting environment that creates our scene.

In the next chapter, we will add a main character to our scene and learn how to create the animations that will bring it to life!

3
Add Some Character

"Animation can explain whatever the mind of man can conceive. This facility makes it the most versatile and explicit means of communication yet devised for quick mass appreciation."

– Walt Disney Company

"Believe in your character. Animate (or write) with sincerity."

– Glen Keane

Overview

In this chapter, we will learn how to add a character to our game using a sprite by covering the following points:

- What is a sprite?
- Creating a sprite
- Importing a sprite
- Slicing sprite sheets
- Texture atlasing
- Sprite Renderer
- Animating a sprite
- Animation Editor
- Dopesheet 2D animations
- Animator

What is a sprite?

A sprite is a 2D image or animation (sequence of images) that we can manipulate on screen. The following image shows an example of a sprite:

Creating a sprite

In order to add a character to our game, we need to either use a pre-existing sprite that we have rights to or create a sprite first.

Image editing software

To create a sprite we will need graphic design software or image editing software, like the one shown in the following screenshot:

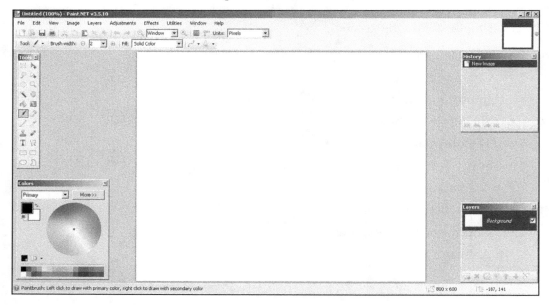

There is a wide and diverse range of software of varying features, ease of use, and prices. The most well-known and widely used image editing software in the game development industry are: Photoshop, Xara, and Paint.NET. Paint.NET is free to use and can be downloaded from `http://www.getpaint.net`.

Once we have downloaded the software, we create our character sprite. A character sprite is a 2D image of a character and can be made of a single image or multiple images. We will create our character from multiple images since it helps when animating the character as the different body parts will be able to move independently.

Sprite sheet

A sprite sheet is an image consisting of separate multiple images. The following screenshot shows a sprite sheet made up of multiple images for the parts of the body:

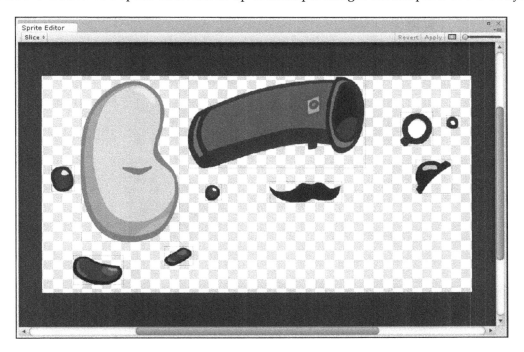

Raster versus vector

When we create a sprite, we need to ensure that we use a raster image as Unity does not support vector images.

A raster image, also known as a bitmap, is an image made up of bits that translates into pixels defined according to a grid of pixel (picture element) color values. Vector images are without grids and use a mathematical formula that defines points and paths that connect to form an image. Thus, when magnified, a raster image looks very pixelated whereas a vector image looks very clear.

The following image clearly shows the difference between a raster image and a vector image:

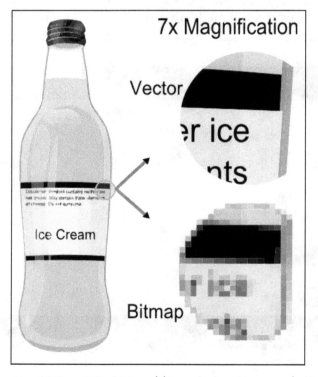

Vector vs raster, viewed 22 June 2014, `http://en.wikipedia.org/wiki/Vector_graphics#mediaviewer/File:VectorBitmapExample.svg`

File formats

Unity supports the following 2D formats: PSD, TIFF, JPG, TGA, PNG, GIF, BMP, IFF, and PICT.

We will make use of PNG because it is the most used, lossless image compression format, and it supports varying levels of alpha transparency per pixel, which can be useful when our sprite features things like tinted glass.

Lossless image compression means that the image does not lose any quality (pixel information) when its size on disk storage (not size in dimensions) has been compressed. Alpha transparency is needed as we want the background to appear through our sprites.

The following image has a checkerboard background (indicating transparency in most applications):

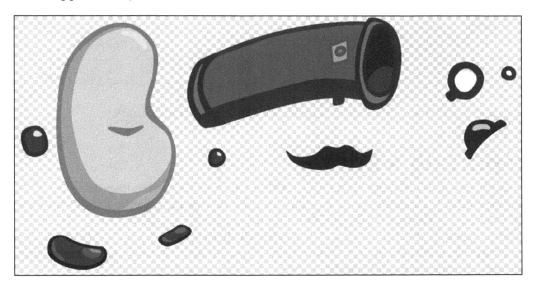

We can get this image from the following URL:

`https://www.assetstore.unity3d.com/#/content/11228`

We save the image in the PNG format as shown in the following screenshot:

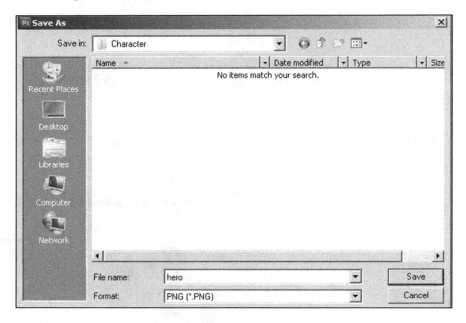

Now that we he have created our sprite, we can import it into Unity.

Importing a sprite

To import a sprite, we repeat the process that we followed when importing a background. We drag the sprite from its location on our PC into the Project Browser and then set its **Texture Type** option to **Sprite** within the Inspector view. The only difference is that this time, we set the **Sprite Mode** drop-down box to **Multiple** since our single character sprite is made up of multiple images. Once we are done setting the import settings, we hit **Apply**.

All the settings are shown in the following screenshot:

Slicing sprite sheets

If we had used a single image in our sprite, then we would not have needed to slice the sprite sheet. As we are using multiple images, we need to slice the sprite sheet to separate the clubbed images into their individual images.

Sprite Editor

To slice a sprite sheet, we need to open the Sprite Editor either by selecting **Sprite Editor** within the **Inspector** toolbar during Import settings or by first selecting the image in the Project Browser as shown in the following screenshot:

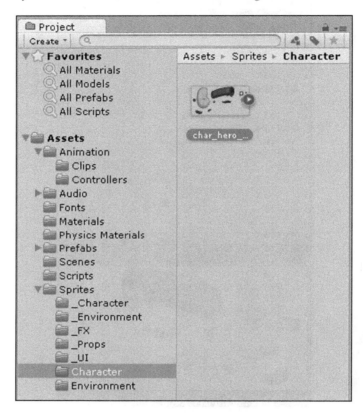

We then navigate to **Window | Sprite Editor** as shown in the following screenshot:

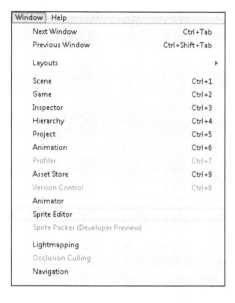

Manual slicing

To slice each image into its own sprite manually, we first drag and select the image within the **Sprite Editor** window. A blue selection area box will then be displayed as shown in the following screenshot:

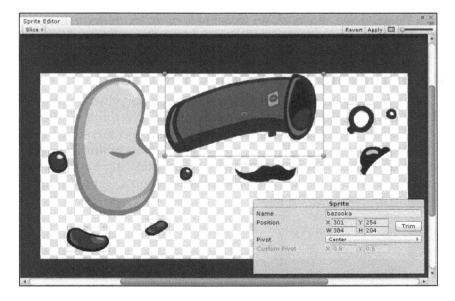

We resize the selection area by dragging and moving the handles on the corners of the box to fit around one of the multiple images. We do the same for all the other images within the sprite sheet. We can also name, set the size, and position the box within the **Sprite** box as shown in the following screenshot (Unity only supports rectangular sprite cuts):

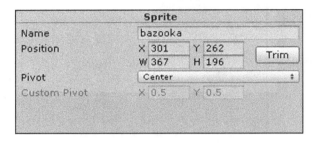

We need to name our sprites as we will refer to them when animating them and coding scripts. This also makes it easier and clearer to view and find the sprite within the scene and hierarchy. We can enter the x and y coordinates as well as the width and height that we would like for the selection area within the **Sprite** settings. We can also trim the selection area by clicking on the **Trim** button. This will resize the selection area to surround the image much closer, removing unnecessary space.

Lastly, we can set the pivot location for the selection area by selecting our choice from the drop-down box and then clicking on **Apply** at the top-right corner of **Sprite Editor**.

Pivots are used to define the center position of a sprite and also its center of rotation. The **Custom Pivot** choice allows a user to define a pivot location on the sprite that offers more flexibility when needed.

Adding and removing a selection area

To create a new selection area, we simply click and hold anywhere within the sprite sheet and then drag. A green selection area will appear. The more we drag, the larger the size of the selection area. Once we release the mouse and therefore the selection area, it will turn blue to indicate that we have created the selection area. We can then resize and edit if we need to do any tweaks to it. The following screenshot shows a new selection area being created with the green selection area box being dragged to surround the moustache of the character:

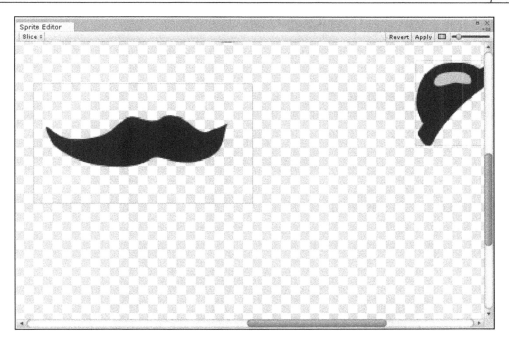

To remove a selection area, we simply select the one that we would like to remove and then press the *Delete* button on our keyboard.

Toolbar controls

The top-right corner of the **Sprite Editor** window consists of a colored bar button, which enables us to toggle the view of the image and its alpha channels. It also contains a slider bar that controls the level of magnification of the image.

There are also the **Revert** and **Apply** buttons that allow us to apply or revert all of our changes within the **Sprite Editor** window. The following is a screenshot displaying the toolbar controls at the top-right corner:

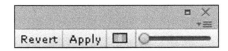

Automatic slicing

To save us time, Unity provides several options for the automatic slicing of the sprite sheet.

The following screenshot shows the **Slice** drop-down box, which is at the top-left corner of the screen and is used for automatic slicing:

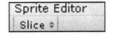

Slicing type – automatic

To automatically slice our sprite sheet, we click on the **Slice** drop-down box, which provides us with the options shown in the following screenshot:

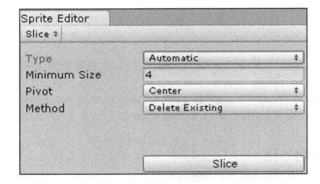

We leave the **Type** drop-down box at its default option as **Automatic** as we simply want to slice our sprite sheet automatically.

When set to **Automatic**, Unity decides where to place the selection area boxes that separate the multiple images based on the full transparency surrounding the images. It can tell where an image is by checking whether each pixel within the image is opaque or slightly transparent; otherwise, if it is fully transparent, Unity can tell that it is not part of the image and therefore surrounds it.

As Unity can pick up very tiny pixels surrounded by transparent space, we can increase the value of the **Minimum Size** box to ensure that it does not create many tiny selection area boxes selecting tiny details individually. Therefore we will set the value of **Minimum Size** to 4.

We can set the pivots for the automatically generated selection areas by selecting the **Pivot** drop-down box. We will leave it at its default value **Center** as it is the most used option and the easiest to work with.

The **Method** drop-down box has three settings as shown in the following screenshot:

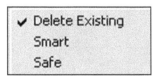

If we created selection areas manually before selecting the automatic option, then with the **Delete Existing** option, it will delete all the existing selection areas and then add the newly created automatic selection areas.

The **Smart** option will either try to keep the existing selection areas or edit them while also adding new selection area boxes.

The **Safe** option will add new selection areas together with the existing ones and keep the pre-existing selection area boxes exactly as they are.

To ensure that we are only using automatic slicing, we will select **Delete Existing** as our **Method** option.

Slicing type – grid

When we use a sprite sheet that is divided into equally sized images, then we use the grid type for automatic slicing as this speeds up the image slicing process significantly.

We will most certainly use this when animating our sprites as shown in the following screenshot, whereby the sprite sheet is comprised of the character's walk animation:

 We can download the image from the following URL:
`http://freeartsprites.com/rougelike-2/`

When we select the **Grid** option from the **Type** drop-down box, then we are presented with the following screenshot:

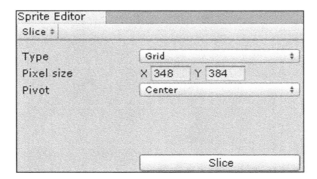

The **Pixel size** setting allows us to set the *x* and *y* coordinates for the selection areas of each individual image. Once we are satisfied with the sizes, we press the **Slice** button. These sizes will get repeated as a grid over the image within the **Sprite Editor** window as shown in the following screenshot:

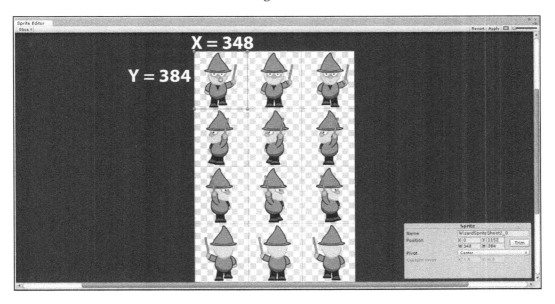

Once we are satisfied with the automatic slicing, we click on the **Apply** button (under the toolbar controls previously mentioned) to confirm and slice up the single image into multiple sprites.

To view the separated images, we click on the arrow beside the original sprite sheet within the Project Browser as shown in the following screenshot:

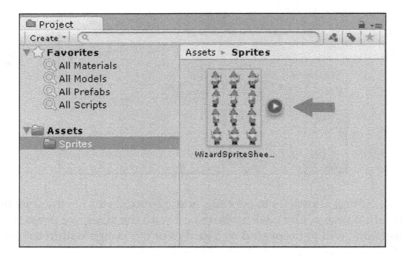

Upon clicking on the arrow, the Project Browser will display the multiple separated sprite assets we have created as displayed in the following screenshot:

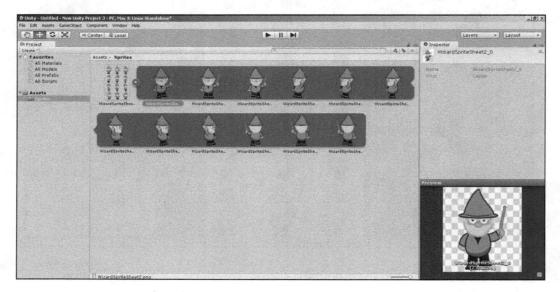

Texture atlasing

When working with sprites, it is easier and more convenient to use a separate image (otherwise known as a texture file) for each character. However, the image will usually have a lot of empty space surrounding it, and this takes up video memory during runtime (when the game is running), which impacts performance. In order to reduce the wastage and optimize performance, we make use of texture atlasing. A technique called **draw call batching** that Unity and other engines use also helps to improve the frame rate. It too requires texture atlasing particularly for PC games, whereby a complex 2D scene would probably become CPU-bound.

What is a texture atlas?

A texture atlas packs several separate images (textures) into a single texture. The following is an image representing a texture file that does not use texture atlasing:

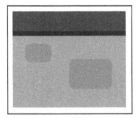

The following image represents a texture file using a texture atlas:

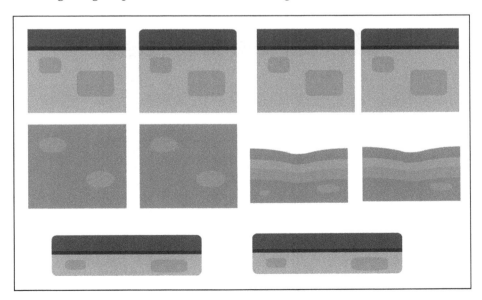

Sprite packer

To create a texture atlas, Unity now supports a sprite packer; however, this feature is only available in the Pro version.

As texture atlasing is a pro feature, and the sprite packer makes it straightforward as it automates the process for us, we will not go into the details of all the extra settings.

Basically, in order to convert our separate texture files into texture atlases, we open up the sprite packer window by going to the main toolbar and navigating to **Window | Sprite Packer** as shown in the following screenshot:

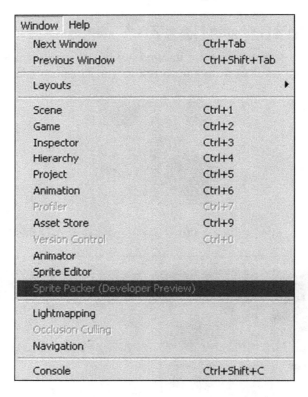

The following screenshot displays the **Sprite Packer** window with all its options:

http://docs.unity3d.com/uploads/Main/SpritePackerMain.png.

When we click on the **Pack** button at the top-left corner, our texture atlas is created automatically using all the default settings improving performance by saving all the space that would have otherwise been wasted.

Adding our character

Now that we have sliced our sprite sheet and our character sprite assets are ready, we now need to add our character to the game by creating a sprite GameObject.

To do so, we simply drag the selected sprite asset (in this case, we will use the body as our main GameObject) from the Project Browser as shown in the following screenshot:

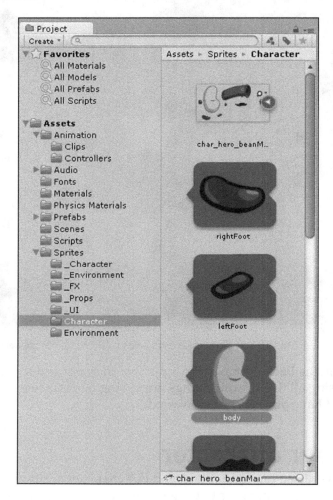

Then, we drop it into the **Hierarchy** tab as shown in the following screenshot:

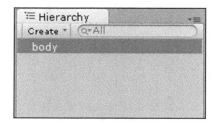

To make it clearer, we rename the body GameObject to a character as it will act as the character GameObject consisting of all the character's body parts.

To rename it, we select the body listed within the Hierarchy and right-click on it. A drop-down box will appear with the option to rename the GameObject as shown in the following screenshot:

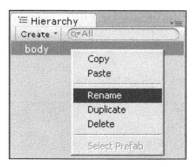

Currently the Scene View should look like the following screenshot:

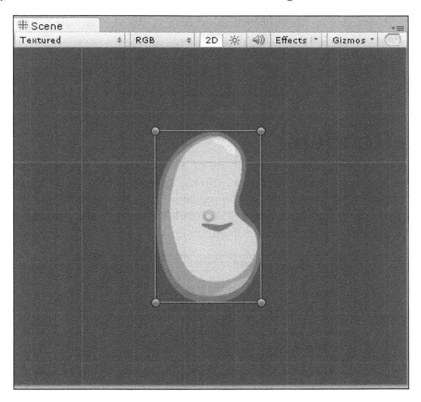

Now that the GameObject appears as a character, we select the remaining body parts that will make up our character from the Project Browser, drag them to the **Hierarchy** tab, and drop them over the character so that the character becomes the parent and all the other parts are the children.

This is to ensure that the body parts are locked to the character and inherit any changes that are applied to the character; for instance, when we move the character, all the parts move relative to the character. Otherwise, any position change with the character would have resulted with the need to change all the positions of each and every body part.

The **Hierarchy** tab should now look as follows:

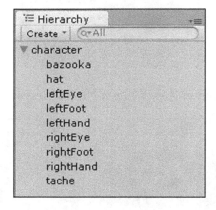

Sprite Renderer

When we select the character parent or any of its children, the **Sprite Renderer** component will display this selection within the **Inspector** toolbar. It contains all the settings that affect how the image will be rendered (in other words, how the image's appearance is displayed). The following screenshot shows us the **Sprite Renderer** component in Unity:

The **Sprite** field contains the reference to the sprite asset that the GameObject is using. Should we want to replace the image that the GameObject is using, we simply need to click on the circle (highlighted) as in the following screenshot:

This will open the sprite asset folder allowing us to pick any asset that we have added to our project. This is shown in the following screenshot:

The **Color** field is a blend mode that multiplies the color selected with the sprite's original color. As we would like to keep the sprite's original color, we leave this setting at the default white. If we wanted to change the color, we simply click on the color box or color picker next to it.

The **Material** field allows us to select the material we would like to use, which affects the image's rendering properties as well as the assets used. We can leave this as the default material. If we want to change it, we can simply click on the circle beside the setting, which will open the material asset folder.

The **Sorting Layer** option is where we group a selection of sprites that we want to display on the same layer. We will leave this at its default settings.

The **Order in Layer** option specifies which order we want the selected layer to appear. As we want the body of the character to appear in front of the bazooka, we leave the bazooka's **Order in Layer** option to **0** and set the character's **Order in Layer** option to **1**. Depending on the order, we drag the parts we may need to adjust the **Order in Layer** option of a few of the other parts.

We will now need to move the body parts of the character within the Scene View so that they appear in the correct positions. The result should appear as shown in the following screenshot:

Animating a sprite

Now that we have added our character to the scene, we want to bring it to life by animating the sprite.

To do so, we select our character in the Scene View or from the **Hierarchy** tab and open the **Animation Editor** window by going to the main toolbar and navigating to **Window | Animation** as shown in the following screenshot:

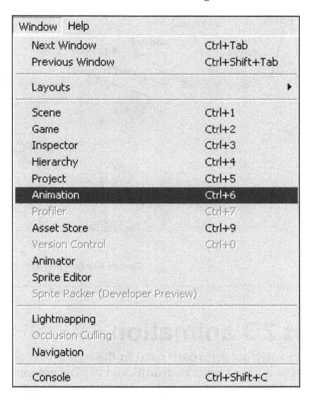

Animation Editor

Within the Animation Editor, we can set up our dopesheet 2D animations using frames on the timeline and curves that we will add. The following screenshot represents the Animation Editor with the interface clearly labeled as we will refer to each of the tools when creating our animation:

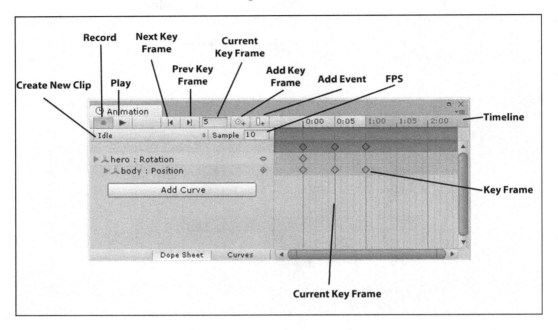

Dopesheet 2D animation

Dopesheet is the user-interface approach used in the editor to create animation clips. The word Dopesheet is derived from its traditional use in cartoons and film/TV. Similar to a storyboard, it is used in planning animations using frames and sections.

To create a reusable animation clip for our character of it breathing, follow these steps:

1. We select the character, click on the **Create New Clip** drop-down box, and then click on **Create New Clip**.
2. We then select `Idle` as the name of our animation and click on **Save**.
3. Now we select **Add Curve**.
4. A drop-down box will appear giving us several options.

5. We click on **Transform** to open all the transform properties and then select **Position** by clicking on the plus button next to it as shown in the following screenshot:

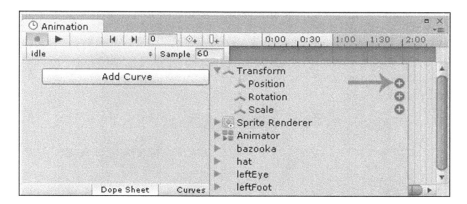

6. We will animate our character breathing by moving its body's position up and down slightly.

7. We need to reduce the **frames per second** (**FPS**) from 60 down to 10 so that the animation is slower and smoother as this property controls how many frames are played per second.

8. The record button should already be pressed down when the button is red because adding a new curve automatically enables recording. If we have accidentally disabled it, we press the record button and move our character up slightly in the Scene View or the Inspector to change its position for the first frame. This will add a key to the frame resulting in a key frame. When moving our character within the Scene View, we can hold the *Shift* key while dragging to ensure that we move it in a straight path and the *Ctrl* key snaps the sprite along a grid defined in **Edit | Snap Settings**.

9. We then type 5 within the current key frame to add a new key frame, and move the character down again.

10. Finally we add 10 to the current key frame and move the character up once again to add the final key frame.

11. We then click on the record button to stop recording and press play to view our animation. We must not forget to stop recording! Otherwise, we will inadvertently record things in our animation that we did not mean to.

12. To delete any key frames, click on the key frames to select them, and then press *Delete*.

13. Now when we play our game from the Game View, we will see our character animating — our character is alive!

Animator

The Animator allows us to switch between multiple animations (or states) when certain game conditions occur. For example, when a character is in a jumping state, Unity will automatically enable the jump animation. We define which character states correspond to the animations in the Animator View.

1. To open the Animator, we go to the main toolbar and navigate to **Window | Animator**. The **Animator** Window will open and look as follows:

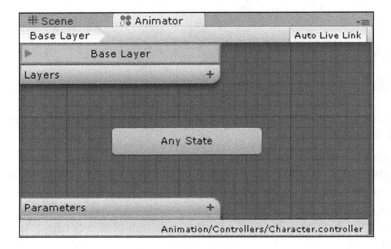

2. Now, we add our character's idle animation to the Animator by simply dragging the idle animation from the Project Browser and dropping it into the Animator View.

3. We then right-click on the **Any State** option within the Animator, select **Make Transition**, and then click on the idle animation state. We now have the any state transitioning into the idle animation.

4. We use **Any State** when we want to jump to a state (an animation to play) no matter what state our character is in.

5. We then right-click on the **idle** state and select **Set As Default** to set the idle state to run when we first run the game. By default, this should already be the case, and therefore, **Set As Default** will be grayed out but is worth noting in case we accidentally set a different animation state as default.

The Animator View should now look as follows:

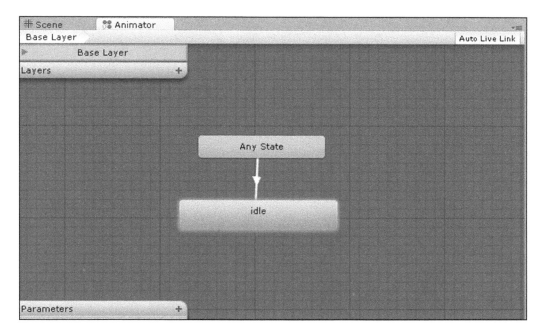

Run the scene/game by pressing play in the Game View to see our character come alive!

Summary

In this chapter, we learned to create and add characters to our games using sprites by creating, importing, slicing, and animating sprites.

In the next chapter, we will learn how to not only bring our character to life, but all the elements in the game through coding. We will go through the foundations of coding so that we can make use of the basic building blocks to bring our ideas to life.

4
Code Control

"The most important property of a program is whether it accomplishes the intention of its user."

– C.A.R. Hoare

"The computer programmer is a creator of universes for which he alone is the lawgiver. No playwright, no stage director, no emperor, however powerful, has ever exercised such absolute authority to arrange a stage or field of battle and to command such unswervingly dutiful actors or troops."

– Joseph Weizenbaum

Overview

In this chapter, we will learn the core concepts of programming by creating basic code in the UnityScript that will take us from printing output and controlling a character to destroying an enemy.

Here's a list of topics that will be covered in this chapter:

- Why do we need code?
- Code fundamentals
- Hello world
- Controlling the character
- Destroying the enemy
- Coroutines
- Namespaces
- Unity Scripting Reference

Why do we need code?

In order to create any type of game, we need to understand code because the pieces of code are the instructions that tell the game engine (Unity) when and how you want something to occur at any given point.

Programming languages

In order to create code, we use a programming language, which is an intermediary language that represents the instructions that we tell the computer processor.

Levels of programming languages

There are three levels of programming languages:

- Machine language
- Assembly language
- High-level languages

Machine language

Computers do not understand human language; therefore, we need to communicate with the computer processor via machine language.

Machine language, also known as binary code, consists of a combination of 0s and 1s that represent high and low electrical voltages. These 0s and 1s are known as **bits** (**binary digits**). We can then make use of data by representing the data using these bits.

All data has an area on the computer or device where it is stored (known as the memory address) as well as the actual data stored (known as memory content). The computer or device then uses the memory address to find where the data is stored so that it can access the memory content.

Binary code can also be represented in hexadecimal format, whereby each hexadecimal digit represents four binary digits. The hexadecimal format is shorthand and a more human-friendly representation of binary code.

All programs and thus games must be converted into machine language before they can be executed.

The following table is a visual representation of machine language, showing both the binary and hexadecimal representations:

Machine Language			
Memory Address		**Memory Content**	
Binary	**HEX**	**Binary**	**HEX**
0000000000000000	0000	11011011	DB
0000000000000001	0001	00000100	04
0000000000000010	0002	11000110	C6

Assembly language

Assembly is a low-level language that uses symbolic operation code that assigns human-readable names to each instruction from machine language to represent machine language. It is extremely fast to run; however, it's much more difficult to learn, and it takes significantly longer to write with many more lines of code than high-level languages.

The following code is a representation of assembly language:

```
;Example of Assembly language
;Accepts a number in the register AX;
;Subtracts 50 if it is in the range 100-150;
;Else it remains as it is.

SUB50   PROC
    CMP AX,100
    JL DONE
    CMP AX,150
    JG DONE
    SUB AX,50
DONE:   RET
SUB50   ENDP
```

High-level languages

High-level languages are programming languages that use statements that are closer to the English language and are therefore easier to learn.

The following code is a representation of Java—a high-level language:

```
/*Example of subtraction in Java
*The resulting values are then displayed
*/
public class Subtraction
{

    public static void main(String[] args)
    {
        int number1 = 100;
        int number2 = 50;

        //calculating number1 - number2;
        int difference = number1 - number2;


        //Displaying the values
        System.out.println("number1 : "+number1);
        System.out.println("number2 : "+number2);
        System.out.println("difference : "+difference);

    }
}
```

Scripting languages

Scripting languages are an alternative to programming languages, whereby we create lightweight, much more human-readable scripts that are interpreted by another program at runtime rather than compiled by the computer's processor directly as compiled languages are. Thus, scripting languages are normally slower than compiled languages.

Modern languages, such as UnityScript, make use of both. UnityScript, although a scripting language providing flexibility, gets compiled, making it much faster.

The following diagram shows the layers/levels of programming languages:

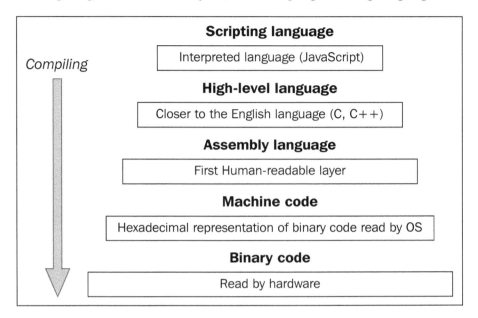

UnityScript versus C# versus Boo

When programming code for our game in Unity, there are three languages that we can choose from: UnityScript, C#, and Boo.

All of them are relatively equal, and the choice in language depends on which one you are more familiar with, for example:

- If you come from a background programming in C++ and Java, then you will find C# more familiar
- If you have experience in PHP, BASIC, or JavaScript, then you will prefer UnityScript. UnityScript is Unity's version of the widely used scripting language JavaScript with several differences.
- If you are completely new to programming, then UnityScript is the easiest to pick up and learn quickly. You do not need to worry about types and casting as UnityScript handles it automatically for you.

The following script represents code written in UnityScript:

```
// Message with a link to an object.
Debug.Log ("Hello", gameObject);

// Message using rich text.
Debug.Log("<color=red>Fatal error:</color>
  AssetBundle not found");
```

Beginners may find C# more daunting, but it is more powerful, better suited for games requiring networking features, and better for performance.

The following script represents the preceding code written in C#:

```
using UnityEngine;
using System.Collections;

public class ExampleClass : MonoBehaviour {
    void Example() {
        Debug.Log("Hello", gameObject);
        Debug.Log("<color=red>Fatal error:</color> AssetBundle not
found");
    }
}
```

Boo is not widely used. However, if you are familiar with the Python language syntax, then you may prefer to use Boo.

The following script represents the same preceding code written in Boo:

```
import UnityEngine
import System.Collections

public class ExampleClass(MonoBehaviour):

  def Example() as void:
    Debug.Log('Hello', gameObject)
    Debug.Log('<color=red>Fatal error:</color> AssetBundle not
  found')
```

As this book is aimed at beginners, we will make use of UnityScript in all our code throughout the book.

Code fundamentals

In order to create our own code, we need to understand the foundations of programming so that we can build upon it.

Code is made up of the following main components:

- Variables
- Data types
- Operators (also known as expressions)
- Functions (also known as methods)
- Comments
- Library import variables

When programming, we make use of variables to store both known and unknown information in the form of values and identifiers in named locations in memory.

For instance, we could store the name of the main character in our game in a variable, as shown in the following line of code:

```
Name = Hercules
```

`Name` is the variable's identifier, and `Hercules` is the stored value assigned to the variable `Name`.

Data types

Variables are used in programming to store different types of data. Setting the variable type is known as **Typing**. The reason to use types and type checking is that expressions involving incompatible types can be detected right away rather than becoming hidden bugs (errors in code). For instance, if we are attempting to perform calculations and we accidentally assign a `string` (text) value to a variable of type `int` (integer number), then an error will appear as soon as we try to build our script, whereas if we did not use types and type checking, then the script would have attempted to do a calculation with the text, which would produce nonsensical output.

There are many data types in Unity. The most commonly used variable types in UnityScript are:

Data type	Variable data
String	Text within double quotes such as "Press start to play."
Integer (written as `int`)	A whole number such as 3.
Float	A number with a decimal point such as 3.14159.
Boolean	True or False.
GameObject	An object in a Unity scene. It contains all the data that makes up an object, such as its name, position, and so on.

To declare and initialize a variable, we use the following syntax:

```
var varName:DataType   //assignment operator value
```

The following is an example of the preceding syntax:

```
var playerAmmo:Int = 3;
```

Declaring a variable simply means that we are announcing the existence of an element, be it an object, piece of text, number, and so on, by typing out what it is, which, in this case, is a variable with its name, type, and value.

Initializing means that we are assigning a value to the variable from the start—its initial value.

The preceding code creates a variable of type integer that stores the amount of player ammunition and in this case has an initial amount of 3.

Operators

Operators are symbols which operate on variables. There are several kinds of operators. The most commonly used operators are assignment, arithmetic, relational, and logical operators.

Assignment operator	Meaning	Example
=	Stores a value into a variable	A = 72

Arithmetic operators	Meaning	Example
+	Addition	A = 5 + 4 (A=9)
-	Subtraction	A = 10-5 (A=5)
*	Multiplication	A = 5*2 (A=10)
/	Division	A = 10/2 (A=5)
%	Remainder after division	A = 10%3 (A=1)

Relational operators	Meaning	Example
>	Greater than	7>3 True
<	Smaller than	7<3 False
>=	Greater than or equal to	7>=3 True
<=	Smaller than or equal to	3<=3 True
==	Equal to	7==3 False
!=	Not equal to	3!=7 True

Logical operators	Meaning	Example
||	Logical OR	a=1 and b=2 If ((a==1)||(b<1)) returns true
&&	Logical AND	a=1 and b=2 If ((a==1)&&(b<1)) returns false
!	Logical NOT	a=1 If !(a==1) returns false

Functions

Functions accomplish a specific task combining multiple instructions into a single line of code. They are called by their name and can be reused as many times as required. Functions are triggered by certain events that we specify.

UnityScript comes with many built-in functions that help make coding many common tasks quicker. UnityScript files come with two required functions by default: Start() and Update(). The Start function has the following syntax:

```
Function Start()
{
}
```

The Start function gets called only once when the script is first enabled on the very first frame. Games and computer programs in general run at a certain number of frames per second. Thus, the Start function gets called on the very first frame during runtime.

This function is useful when we want to initialize—set values to variables at the very start of the game, for example, how many lives the player will start with.

Curly braces/brackets are used to mark when a function begins and when it ends. Every function has to have a start and an end; otherwise, if one is missing, then the code will not work, and it will throw an error on the console when we try to build our code.

The following is the syntax for the Update function:

```
function Update()
{
}
```

Unlike the Start function, the Update function gets called every frame (thus, it will be called several times within a second) and is useful to call functions that we would like to continuously occur, for example, an enemy moving.

To declare a function, we do the following:

```
function FunctionName()
{
}
```

To call a function, we do the following:

```
FunctionName( );
```

To pass a variable to a function to be used with a function, we do the following:

```
function FunctionName(variableName:Int)
{
}

FunctionName(variableName);
```

To pass multiple variables to a function to be used with a function, we do the following:

```
function FunctionName(var1:Int, var2:String)
{
}

FunctionName(var1, var2);
```

To return a variable from a function, we do the following:

```
function FunctionName():Int
{
return variableName;
}

variableName = FunctionName();
```

In UnityScript, variables declared outside a function become member (function) instance variables of the script with a per-instance state, which typically means a per-game-object state; for example:

```
var playerAmmo:Int = 10;
function LevelAmmo ()
{
}
```

If we want all functions in our code to be able to access a variable, then we declare a global variable. To do this, we simply use the `static` keyword when declaring the variable as shown in the following line of code:

```
static var playerAmmo:Int;
```

And then, to access it in the same script, we simply call it:

```
playerAmmo = 1;
```

If we want to use it in another script, we include the name of the script as shown in the following line of code:

```
Scriptname.playerAmmo = 10;
```

However, if we want a variable to only be available to a certain function, then we declare it as a local variable. To do this, we simply declare it within the function like the following code snippet:

```
function LevelAmmo ()
{
var playerAmmo:Int = 10;
}
```

Now, if we scripted another function calling the preceding `playerAmmo` variable, then an error would result since the variable is not within scope, and therefore, the function does not know about it. For example:

```
function CountAmmo()
{
ammoCount = playerAmmo + 1; //error would occur
}
```

When naming functions or variables, we can use alphanumeric characters of upper or lowercase. However, they cannot start with a number. We must remember to use the same case when calling a declared function or variable, else it will not match and we will get an error. This is due to the fact that the same word with a different case is seen as a new and different (unique) variable or function.

We can also use underscores to separate words in a function or variable name, such as `player_Health`. We should not use existing syntax as our function or variable name as it will produce an error, for example, naming a function or variable `function` as shown in the following code:

```
function function()
{
}
```

Conditional statements

When programming, we use a conditional statement to check variables so that we can control the flow of the game and decide on what code to execute at certain points.

If...else

We use the `if...else` conditional statement as follows:

```
if (condition)
{
  //do a certain action
}
else
{
  //otherwise do a different action
}
```

We don't have to always use `else`. For instance, have a look at the following statement:

```
if (playerHealth = = 0)
{
  gameOver = true;
}
```

As the game will continue when `playerHealth` is not equal to zero, we need not add the `else` statement.

Using comments

We add comments to our code to make it clearer and much easier to understand when we return to it, to remind ourselves. Comments are also used when working with other people in a team as they will need to understand our code and we, theirs.

To add a comment to our code, we add double forward slashes before our comment as shown in the following syntax:

```
//This is a comment
```

Classes

A class is a template to create objects by specifying a set of variables and functions. The objects are instances of a class.

Think of a class as a template, blueprint, or factory (not to be confused with the advanced object-oriented design pattern used in programming) that creates objects.

You could have a class bicycle, and the objects based on that class would be the different types of bicycles, such as a racing bike, dirt bike, and hybrid bike.

The following is an example of a class in UnityScript:

```
class Bicycle {

// fields are public by default
var type : String;

function Bicycle(x : int) {
      this.type = ["racing bike", "dirt bike", "hybrid bike"] [x];
  }
  function announce() {
     print("I am a "+this.type+".");
  }
}
```

```
var object = new Bicycle(1);

// prints  "I am a dirt bike." because code lists usually start
   at 0.
object.announce();
```

In fact, the functions that we went through earlier in the chapter, if simply placed in a UnityScript file, are part of an implicit class that Unity creates for us. The class name is taken automatically from the name of the UnityScript file.

Private versus public

Variables and functions within classes have two levels of scope and accessibility:

- Private
- Public

Private functions and variables can only be accessed by other functions within the same class. Public functions and variables can be accessed by functions within the same class as well as other classes.

To declare a variable or function, either private or public, we use the following syntax:

```
Public var varName:DataType = value;
Private var varName:DataType = value;

Public function FunctionName( )
{
}

Private function FunctionName( )
{
}
```

Importing external libraries

When we want to make use of external libraries (for instance, third-party tools, classes, **Software Development Kits (SDKs)**, and **Application Programming Interfaces (APIs)**), we first need to import them by adding the word import followed by the name of the external library that we would like to import, as shown in the following code statement:

```
import LibraryName;
```

Code editor

To create code, we can simply use a text editor, such as Notepad. However, its simplicity and lack of features makes it much harder and slower to code as well as more error prone. For example, it does not highlight the different entities nor does it provide line numbers.

An integrated development environment (also known as an IDE) is an application that facilitates coding and usually comprises a code editor together with debugging and automation tools.

There are many IDEs available with varying features. Fortunately, Unity comes with the MonoDevelop IDE. MonoDevelop is a feature-rich, cross-platform IDE that makes it easier to port code from one language into another. Thus, we will be using MonoDevelop throughout the book when creating our code.

To open MonoDevelop, we will need to do the following within Unity:

1. Create a new folder by going to the Project Browser and clicking on **Assets** and right-clicking on **Assets**.
2. Then, go to **Create | Folder**.
3. Name the folder `Code`.
4. Now click on the folder to select it. It should be highlighted and empty.
5. Right-click on the empty folder and go to **Create | Javascript**.
6. Name the new file `HelloWorld`.
7. Double-click on the `HelloWorld` file. This should open the MonoDevelop IDE and should look similar to the following screenshot:

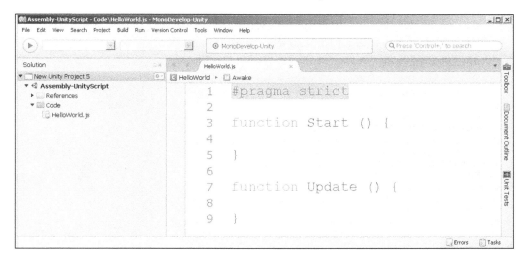

The first line, `#pragma strict`, means that we are enforcing typing where we need to explicitly state what type a variable is. We can remove it if we do not want to have to state each variable type; however, that would be risky as it will be more easily prone to error.

Hello world

When creating our first code, the tradition is to create "hello world" as our very first code. To do this, we need to do the following:

1. In MonoDevelop, within the file we have just created and named `HelloWorld`, we create a variable under `#pragma strict`.

2. To create a variable, we declare it by typing `var`.

3. Follow this by typing `greeting`—the name of the variable.

4. Then, we use a colon `:` to declare the type that the variable will be using, followed by typing out the string type `String` as we want to store text in our variable. We need to ensure that we use `String` with an uppercase *S*; otherwise, we will get an error.

5. We then use the assignment operator `=` followed by the text `"Hello World!"` with quotes to assign the variable with text and thus initialize it.

6. We always finish a line with a semicolon `;`.

7. We then use the UnityScript function `print` by typing out "print" to print out our text, and we pass it the variable we just created so that it will print the information stored within the variable: `print(greeting);`. We place this line of code within the `Start()` function as we want to call it on the very first frame.

8. Our code should look like the following (the code that is highlighted is the code we have just added to the existing script):

```
#pragma strict

var greeting:String = "Hello World!";

function Start ()
{
   print(greeting);
}

function Update ()
{
}
```

9. We now go to **Build | Build All** and should not get any errors. The following screenshot displays the location:

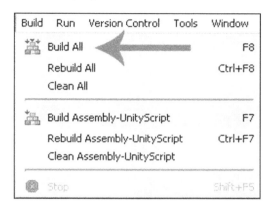

 Running a build in MonoDevelop for Unity is not for the same reason as in other IDEs. Unity (the editor) does the real build automatically once any source changes are detected and the user has focused (pressed *Alt + Tab*) back to the Unity Editor. The **Build** command in MonoDevelop produces output that Unity Editor ignores. Building in MonoDevelop is only useful to help catch build errors without having to switch back to Unity Editor.

10. Back in Unity, we create a new empty GameObject by going to **GameObject | Create Empty**.

11. Now, we assign the script that we just created to the GameObject so that it can be used in our project. To do this, we click on our GameObject to select it and then drag our new script called `HelloWorld` into the Inspector.

12. We open the Console View by going to **Window | Console**.

13. We can now push play and should see the text **Hello World!** displayed in the Console View.

    We should now see the following screenshot:

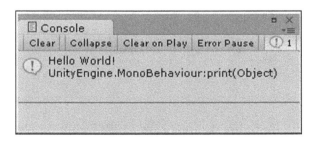

Controlling the character

We are now going to create a script that will enable us to control our character.

We do not build our scripts until we have added all of them as some of them may need to communicate with each other and we will get errors when they do not exist yet and are therefore unknown. Also, we do not actually need to build the scripts as Unity automatically does this. However, it is good practice as it helps to check for errors.

We will control a spaceship, moving it left and right. The following are the steps to do this:

1. Download the free public domain spaceship art from the following URL:

   http://freeartsprites.com/free-art/Space-Pack/

2. We will use the Rocket.png asset as our character sprite.

3. Create a new sprite GameObject, name it Ship, and assign the Rocket.png file shown in the following image as the sprite:

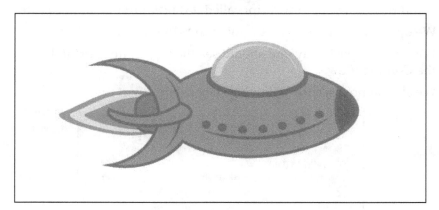

4. Create a folder by right-clicking in the Project Browser and going to **Create | Folder**. Name the folder Code.

5. Create a new script in our `Code` folder and go to **Create | Javascript**.

6. Name it `ControlCharacter`.

7. Add the following code snippet (excluding the text in the information boxes):

 Ensure strict typing—if you use the same variable for different data types, then an error will be thrown when building the script, otherwise these bugs could go unknown.

```
#pragma strict
```

 The speed that the ship will move is declared next.

```
var speed:float = 3.0;


function Start ()
{

}
```

 Move the character each frame.

```
function Update ()
{
  MoveCharacter();
}
```

 We will now look at the function to move characters.

```
function MoveCharacter()
{
```

 If we press *A*, then the ship moves to the left-hand side.

```
if (Input.GetKey(KeyCode.A))
{
  transform.Translate(Vector3.left * speed *
Time.deltaTime);
}
```

 If we press *D*, then the ship moves to the right-hand side.

```
if (Input.GetKey(KeyCode.D))
{
  transform.Translate(Vector3.right * speed * Time.deltaTime);
}
}
```

We then build our script in Unity; we select the character that we created and drag our new script onto its Inspector.

Now when we press play, we can move the spaceship left and right by pressing the *A* and *D* keys respectively.

Destroying the enemy

We are now going to destroy an enemy by spawning laser beams when we fire our spaceship. We will then use collision detection to detect when the laser beams hit the enemy ship. As soon as the enemy ship is hit, it will be destroyed.

We start a new project and add the spaceship image Rocket.png that we used previously; we will now add laser beams by using the following image:

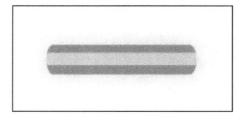

Let's destroy the enemy by executing the following steps:

1. Create a new GameObject and assign the laserbeam sprite to it.
2. Name this GameObject Bullet.
3. Place it behind the spaceship.

4. Select it, and within the Inspector, tag it by going to **Tag | Untagged** and then going to **Tag | Add Tag...**.

5. Name the tag `Bullet` within the **Element 0** field.

6. We must make sure that we then select the **Bullet** tag we just created from the **Tag** drop-down box.

7. Now, go to **Add Component | Physics 2D | Box Collider 2D**.

8. Go to **Add Component | Physics 2D | Rigidbody 2D**.

9. Make sure the **Is Kinematic** option is unchecked (and therefore false) and is thus set to dynamic.

The following screenshot displays a table that explains which colliders work with each other:

	Static Collider	Rigidbody Collider	Kinematic Rigidbody Collider	Static Trigger Collider	Rigidbody Trigger Collider	Kinematic Rigidbody Trigger Collider
Collision detection occurs and messages are sent upon collision						
Static Collider		Y				
Rigidbody Collider	Y	Y	Y			
Kinematic Rigidbody Collider		Y				
Static Trigger Collider						
Rigidbody Trigger Collider						
Kinematic Rigidbody Trigger Collider						

Collision Detection Table, viewed February 20, 2014, `http://docs.unity3d.com/Documentation/Components/class-BoxCollider.html`

Attach the following script to **Ship** by either dragging the script onto the **Ship** GameObject or by selecting the **Ship** GameObject from the scene and then, within the Inspector, going to **Add Component | New Script**.

 Name the script `Spawn.js`. We declare our `bullet` variable of type `Rigidbody2D` in the next line of code.

```
var bullet:Rigidbody2D;
```

 The speed that the bullet will fire at is defined in the next code snippet.

```
var speed:float = 20f;

function Update ()
{
  var bulletInstance:Rigidbody2D;
```

If the fire (*Ctrl* or mouse click) button is pressed and there are no collisions…

```
if(Input.GetButtonDown("Fire1")&& Hit.hit == false)
{
```

 Let's instantiate the bullet facing right and set its velocity to the right. Name all the instances `Bullet`.

```
bulletInstance = Instantiate(bullet, transform.position,
  Quaternion.Euler(new Vector3(0,0,0)));
bulletInstance.velocity = new Vector2(speed, 0);
bulletInstance.name = "Bullet";
    }
}
```

Assign the bullet as the `Rigidbody2D` variable within the Spaceship's Inspector by clicking on the circular button shown in the following screenshot:

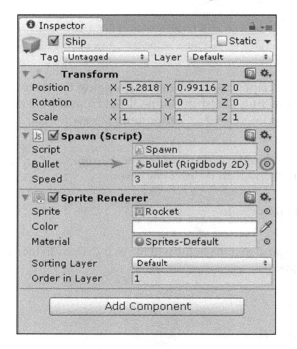

Now we add the enemy spaceship. Go to **Add Component** | **Physics 2D** | **Box Collider 2D**.

Add the following image:

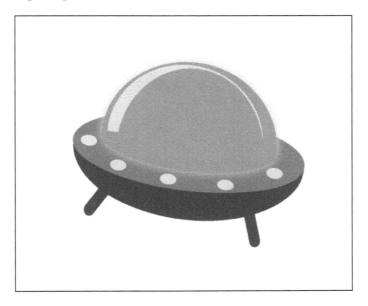

We attach the following new script to the enemy ship:

 Name the script `Hit.js`.
Now, let's make a list of GameObjects.

```
var gameObjects : GameObject[];
```

 A Boolean variable to track when a collision has occurred is defined next.

```
static var hit:boolean = false;
```

Next, we use a function to remove all objects after a collision.

```
function Removal()
{
//Find all bullet objects
    gameObjects =  GameObject.FindGameObjectsWithTag("Bullet");
```

> Next, we use a loop to go through and destroy all bullet objects in the scene.

```
    for(var i = 0 ; i < gameObjects.length ; i ++)
        Destroy(gameObjects[i]);
}
```

> A special Unity function to detect 2D collisions is used now.

```
function OnCollisionEnter2D(other:Collision2D){
```

> Check whether the bullet or bullet clones collide with the enemy.

```
if(other.gameObject.name=="Bullet")
{
```

> Destroy the enemy ship.

```
        Removal();
        Destroy(gameObject);
        hit = true;
    }
}
```

We now build the script that we created and then press play in Unity to test out our script. We either press the *Ctrl* (fire) key or the right mouse button to shoot and destroy the enemy ship.

Coroutines

When we call a function, it runs to completion within a single frame. Therefore, we will create a function that makes an enemy ghost gradually disappear by doing the following:

```
function Fading()
{
  for (var f = 1.0; f >= 0; f -= 0.1)
  {
    var colour = renderer.material.color;
    colour.alpha = f;
    renderer.material.color = colour;
  }
}
```

The preceding code would not give us the result that we were after as is, because it will be completed within one frame. Thus, we will see the ghost enemy disappear instantly.

In order to see the ghost gradually disappear, we would need to see it fade over several frames. To achieve this, we let `yield` do the following:

```
function Fading()
{
  for (var f = 1.0; f >= 0; f -= 0.1)
  {
    var colour = renderer.material.color;
    colour.alpha = f;
    renderer.material.color = colour;
    yield;
  }
}

function Update()
{
  if (Input.GetKeyDown("a"))
  {
    Fading();
  }
}
```

Namespaces

As a game project becomes much larger, it is more likely that you will use the same name for script classes that have similar functions. This results in clashes between the script class names, and therefore, errors when compiling.

This is especially the case when a team of people are working together on a game project as more than one person could think of a certain class name as appropriate. For example, one scripter could be working on the player health, while another scripter is working on the enemy health, and both then decide to call their class `Health`.

To avoid this occurrence, C# offers a feature called namespace that makes use of the namespace as in the following script:

```
namespace Enemy {
  public class Health1 : MonoBehaviour {
    ...
  }

  public class Health2 : MonoBehaviour {
    ...
  }
}
```

Now, when we call our classes, we will use `Enemy.Health1` and `Enemy.Health2`. However, we can avoid having to type `namespace` before each class by adding the `using` directive at the very top line of our script as in the following:

```
using Enemy;
```

Now, we can simply call the classes `Health1` and `Health2` throughout our script.

Unity Scripting Reference

The Unity Scripting Reference is the official central hub of documentation and information for the scripting API that Unity provides. The scripting API is basically a library with specifications (explanations) for the classes and functions of those classes.

The following screenshot shows the Unity Scripting Reference page on the official Unity website:

To access the Unity Scripting Reference, we visit the following URL:

```
https://docs.unity3d.com/Documentation/ScriptReference/index.html
```

UnityScript is also simply called JavaScript by the Unity community and Unity documentation. Within the Unity Scripting Reference, we can search for any terms that we would like to use in our game using the search box, and we can even select the language we would like, as shown in the following screenshot:

The Unity Scripting Reference is very useful and helpful as it also provides snippets of script, as shown in the following screenshot:

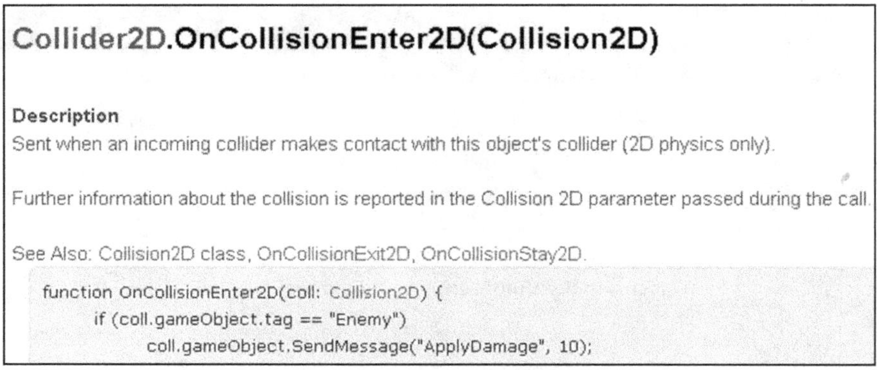

Collider2D.OnCollisionEnter2D(Collision2D)

Description

Sent when an incoming collider makes contact with this object's collider (2D physics only).

Further information about the collision is reported in the Collision 2D parameter passed during the call.

See Also: Collision2D class, OnCollisionExit2D, OnCollisionStay2D.

```
function OnCollisionEnter2D(coll: Collision2D) {
    if (coll.gameObject.tag == "Enemy")
        coll.gameObject.SendMessage("ApplyDamage", 10);
```

Summary

In this chapter, we learned about the core concepts of programming. We created basic code in UnityScript that printed output, controlled a character, and destroyed an enemy.

In the next chapter, we will learn all about the various input types and states. We will then go on to learn how to create buttons and the game controls by using code snippets for input detection.

5
What's Your Input?

"Computers are finite machines; when given the same input, they always produce the same output."

– Greg M. Perry, Sams Teach Yourself Beginning Programming in 24 Hours

Overview

In this chapter, we will learn all about the various input types and states. We will then go on to learn how to create buttons and the game controls by using code snippets for input detection.

The list of topics that will be covered in the chapter is as follows:

- Input versus output
- Input types
- Output types
- Input Manager
- Input detection
- Buttons
- Game controls

Input versus output

We will be looking at exactly what both input and output in games entail. We will look at their functions, importance, and differentiations.

Input in games

Input may not seem a very important part of a game at first glance, but in fact it is very important, as input in games involves how the player will interact with the game. All the controls in our game, such as moving, special abilities, and so forth, depend on what controls and game mechanics we would like in our game and the way we would like them to function.

Most games have the standard control setup of moving your character. This is to help usability, because if players are already familiar with the controls, then the game is more accessible to a much wider audience. This is particularly noticeable with games of the same genre and platform.

For instance, endless runner games usually make use of the *tilt mechanic* which is made possible by the features of the mobile device. However, there are variations and additions to the pre-existing control mechanics; for example, many other endless runners make use of the simple swipe mechanic, and there are those that make use of both.

When designing our games, we can be creative and unique with our controls, thereby innovating a game, but the controls still need to be intuitive for our target players. When first designing our game, we need to know who our target audience of players includes. If we would like our game to be played by young children, for instance, then we need to ensure that they are able to understand, learn, and remember the controls. Otherwise, instead of enjoying the game, they will get frustrated and stop playing it entirely.

As an example, a young player may hold a touchscreen device with their fingers over the screen, thereby preventing the input from working correctly depending on whether the game was first designed to take this into account and support this.

Different audiences of players interact with a game differently. Likewise, if a player is more familiar with the controls on a specific device, then they may struggle with different controls. It is important to create prototypes to test the input controls of a game thoroughly. Developing a well-designed input system that supports usability and accessibility will make our game more immersive.

Output in games

Output is the direct opposite of input; it provides the necessary information to the player. However, output is just as essential to a game as input. It provides feedback to the player, letting them know how they are doing. Output lets the player know whether they have done an action correctly or they have done something wrong, how they have performed, and their progression in the form of goals/missions/objectives.

Without feedback, a player would feel lost. The player would potentially see the game as being unclear, buggy, or even broken. For certain types of games, output forms the heart of the game.

The input in a game gets processed by the game to provide some form of output, which then provides feedback to the player, helping them learn from their actions. This is the cycle of the game's input-output system.

The following diagram represents the cycle of input and output:

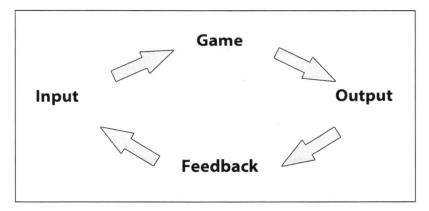

Input types

There are many different input types that we can utilize in our games. These various input types can form part of the exciting features that our games have to offer. The following image displays the different input types:

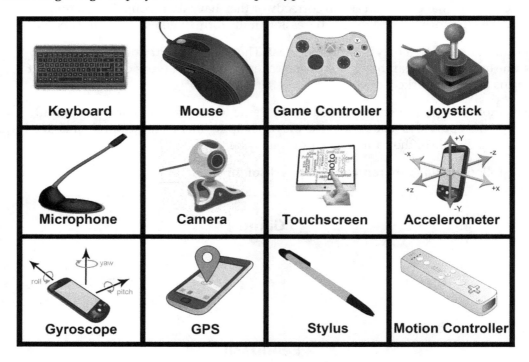

The most widely used input types in games include the following:

- **Keyboard**: Key presses from a keyboard are supported by Unity and can be used as input controls in PC games as well as games on any other device that supports a keyboard.
- **Mouse**: Mouse clicks, motion (of the mouse), and coordinates are all inputs that are supported by Unity.
- **Game controller**: This is an input device that generally includes buttons (including shoulder and trigger buttons), a directional pad, and analog sticks. The game controller input is supported by Unity.

- **Joystick**: A joystick has a stick that pivots on a base that provides movement input in the form of direction and angle. It also has a trigger, throttle, and extra buttons. It is commonly used in flight simulation games to simulate the control device in an aircraft's cockpit and other simulation games that simulate controlling machines, such as trucks and cranes. Modern game controllers make use of a variation of joysticks known as analog sticks and are therefore treated as the same class of input device as joysticks by Unity. Joystick input is supported by Unity.

- **Microphone**: This provides audio input commands for a game. Unity supports basic microphone input. For greater fidelity, a third-party audio recognition tool would be required.

- **Camera**: This provides visual input for a game using image recognition. Unity has webcam support to access RGB data, and for more advanced features, third-party tools would be required.

- **Touchscreen**: This provides multiple touch inputs from the player's finger presses on the device's screen. This is supported by Unity.

- **Accelerometer**: This provides the proper acceleration force at which the device is moved and is supported by Unity.

- **Gyroscope**: This provides the orientation of the device as input and is supported by Unity.

- **GPS**: This provides the geographical location of the device as input and is supported by Unity.

- **Stylus**: Stylus input is similar to touchscreen input in that you use a stylus to interact with the screen; however, it provides greater precision. The latest version of Unity supports the Android stylus.

- **Motion controller**: This provides the player's motions as input. Unity does not support this, and therefore, third-party tools would be required.

Output types

The main output types in games are as follows:

- Visual output
- Audio output
- Controller vibration

Unity supports all three.

Visual output

The **Head-Up Display (HUD)** is the gaming term for the game's **Graphical User Interface (GUI)** that provides all the essential information as visual output to the player as well as feedback and progress to the player as shown in the following image:

HUD, viewed June 22, 2014, http://opengameart.org/content/golden-ui

Other visual output includes images, animations, particle effects, and transitions.

Audio

Audio is what can be heard through an audio output, such as a speaker, to provide feedback that supports and emphasizes the visual output and, therefore, increases immersion. The following image displays a speaker:

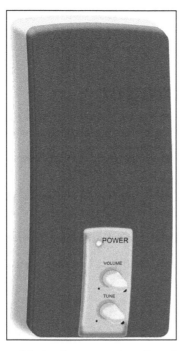

Speaker, viewed June 22, 2014, `http://pixabay.com/en/loudspeaker-speakers-sound-music-146583/`

Controller vibration

Controller vibration provides feedback for instances where the player collides with an object or environmental feedback for earthquakes to provide even more immersion as in the following image:

Having a game that is designed to provide output meaningfully not only makes it clearer and more enjoyable, but can truly bring the world to life, making it truly engaging for the player.

Unity Input Manager

The Input Manager allows us to set up (map) our standard game control configuration for our game, and it has two advantages that are as follows:

- The Input Manager allows us to simply and easily use the default set keys in our scripts
- The Input Manager allows the players of our games to set the controls to their own configurations.

To configure it, we go to **Edit** | **Project Settings** | **Input**.

The following screenshot shows the Input Manager and all the input controls that can be configured:

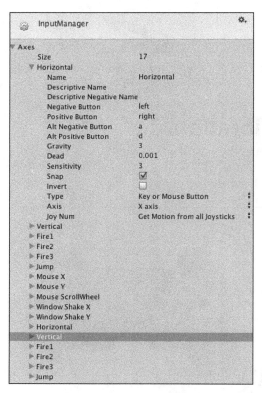

Input Manager, viewed February 25, 2014, `https://docs.unity3d.com/Documentation/Images/manual/class-InputManager-0.jpg`

The following screenshot shows how the Input Manager will be displayed to players of our game from the game launcher:

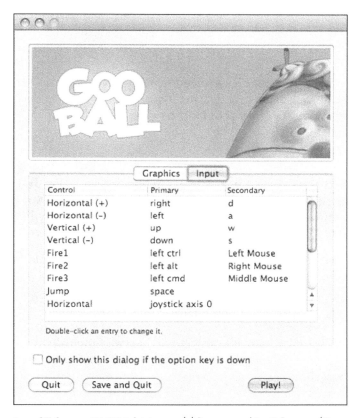

Input Manager, viewed February 25, 2014, `https://docs.unity3d.com/Documentation/Images/manual/class-InputManager-1.jpg`

Detecting input

To detect input from the various devices, namely, computers and mobiles (iOS and Android), we will make use of the Unity class named `Input` with its functions and variables.

For movement-based input, we make use of the `Input.GetAxis()` function to ensure that movement is smoother and to reduce the size and complexity of the script.

For all other action event buttons, we make use of the `Input.GetButton()` function. We always call these functions from within the `Update()` function since they only get reset when the frame updates.

For iOS and Android mobile devices, we can track multiple touch inputs using the `Input.touches` property. We can also track input via the accelerometer and gyroscope using the properties `Input.acceleration` and `Input.gyro` respectively.

Buttons

Usually, the very first input that is required from a player in most games is from buttons on the main menu of a game. Thus, we are now going to create our own buttons using the `OnGui` function provided by Unity.

OnGui

The `OnGUI` function is used for handling GUI events, the creation and the look and functionality of the game's GUI. It is an event function that is part of the well-defined set of callbacks that Unity provides, so it gets called automatically like `Start()` and `Update()`. We, therefore, do not call it within another function.

`OnGUI` can be called several times per frame depending on its implementation. It will get called once per GUI event.

GUILayout.Button

We will use the existing Unity class `GUILayout` and its function `Button` to create our buttons. We specify the text that we would like to display in our buttons as well as our buttons' dimensions as parameters within the function as shown in the following script:

```
function OnGUI()
{
```

 If we click on **Button 1** as input, then we print out the debug text `Button 1 clicked!` to the Console window as output feedback using the `Debug.Log()` function. The `Debug.Log()` function is very useful for debugging/testing our games.

```
if(GUILayout.Button("Button 1",  GUILayout.Width(100),
  GUILayout.Height(100)))
{        Debug.Log("Button 1 clicked!");
  }
```

> If we click on **Button 2** as input, then we print out the debug text
> `Button 2 clicked!` to the Console window as output feedback
> using the `Debug.Log()` function.
>
> The `Debug.Log()` function is very useful for debugging/testing
> our games.

```
    if(GUILayout.Button("Button 2",  GUILayout.Width(100), GUILayout.
Height(100)))
  {
      Debug.Log("Button 2 clicked!");
  }
}
```

We will now perform the following steps:

1. Create a new script by going to **Assets | Create | Javascript**.

2. Name the script `buttons`.

3. Double-click on it to open the script in MonoDevelop.

4. Replace the default existing script with the preceding script.

5. Build our script in MonoDevelop by going to **Build | Build All**.

6. Add the preceding script to an empty GameObject by going to
   GameObject | Create Empty and dragging the script `buttons.js`
   onto the Inspector of the empty GameObject.

7. We should get the result shown in the following screenshot when
   we click on play and click on **Button 1**:

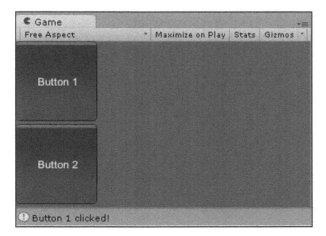

Game controls

In the previous chapter, we learned how to move a character left and right using input from our keyboard. However, many games make use of virtual controls instead, which are onscreen controls. Therefore, it is worth creating our own game controls onscreen as opposed to entering input on the keyboard.

To do this, we will make use of sprites for the HUD to display the virtual controls and raycasting to detect when the player touches a control for input.

Raycasting

Raycasting is a query on the scene that returns objects that intersect with a given ray (which is a point in space with a direction). If we cast a ray from the main 2D camera in a straight line into the screen (specified by where the player is touching/clicking), we can then check if a collider has been hit.

If a collider has been hit, then we can check the name of the collider's GameObject. Depending on which GameObject has been hit, we can call the appropriate script to move the character GameObject in the corresponding direction. Let's use raycasting by executing the given steps:

1. We download some public domain art from the following URL:

   `http://freeartsprites.com/free-art/Space-Pack/`

2. Splice the image so that each control has been separated and the left, right, up, and down portions have become separate sprites.

3. Convert each of these into a GameObject, and name them so that they are identical to the following screenshot:

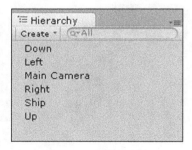

   It is essential that they match as we will be calling those exact names in the script.

4. Add a Box Collider 2D to each control by going to **Add Component |
   Physics 2D | Box Collider 2D**.

5. We are going to check if a collider overlaps a point using
   `Physics2D.OverlapPoint`.

6. Assign the following script to the right control:

 We check which platform the player is using as shown in the
next line of code. We also declare a string variable by the name of
control to store the control object's name.

```
var platform : RuntimePlatform = Application.platform;
```

 We create a function to check for input as shown in the next line
of code.

```
function checkTouch(pos)
{
```

 We use raycasting to detect if the player's finger is overlapping with
the virtual onscreen controls. The first variable is the ray as a 3D
vector as shown in the next line of code.

```
var wp : Vector3 = Camera.main.ScreenToWorldPoint(pos);
```

 The next variable consists of the *x* and *y* coordinates of the player's
finger, which is shown in the next line of code.

```
var touchPos : Vector2 = new Vector2(wp.x, wp.y);
```

 The final variable returns whether or not the player's finger
coordinates overlap with a Physics 2D collider.

```
var hit = Physics2D.OverlapPoint(touchPos);
```

If `hit` returns true, then we move the ship. We also detect which control has received input by checking the name of the object that has received a collision on its collider. We then print it to our log to keep track and then check if the whether it was the right control that was pressed so that we move the ship to the right.

```
if(hit){
    control = hit.transform.name;
    print(""+control);
    if (control == "right")
    {
    move();
    }
    }
}
```

We check to see the device the player is using for input. For instance, if they are using a mobile device, then we use the touch functions for input detection; otherwise, we use the mouse functions for a PC.

With the respective functions, we check when a finger touches the screen for a mobile, or the mouse is pressed down for a PC, and then check the position in coordinates of the finger or mouse.

```
function Update()
{
  if(platform == RuntimePlatform.Android || platform ==
RuntimePlatform.IPhonePlayer){
        if(Input.touchCount > 0) {
            if(Input.GetTouch(0).phase == TouchPhase.Began){
              checkTouch(Input.GetTouch(0).position);
            }
        }
    }else if(platform == RuntimePlatform.WindowsEditor){
        if(Input.GetMouseButtonDown(0)) {
            checkTouch(Input.mousePosition);
        }
    }
}
```

To move our ship, we find the Ship GameObject in the scene by its name. We then move it using `transform.Translate`, which moves the transform in the direction and at the distance of the translation relative to something.

In this case, we translate the ship's position using a 3D vector moving to the right direction multiplied by the distance of 10 units per second moving relative to the camera.

```
function move()
{

    ship = GameObject.Find("Ship");

    ship.transform.Translate(Vector3.right *
    (Time.deltaTime*10), Camera.main.transform);

}
```

7. We will use the ship we used in the previous chapter.

8. When we click on play, the ship should move in the corresponding direction.

9. We copy the script three more times and use exactly the same script that we used before for the left, up, and down controls by simply replacing the direction: `ship.transform.Translate(Vector3.right * (Time.deltaTime*10), Camera.main.transform);`

10. We build our code by going to **Build** | **Build All** and click on the play button in Unity to test it.

The following screenshot displays our ship with virtual controls:

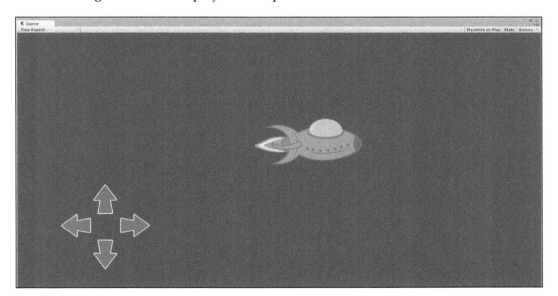

Summary

In this chapter, we learned all about the various input types and states and learned to create buttons as well as the game controls by using code snippets for input detection.

In the next chapter, we will learn how to create our first, basic 2D game in Unity with UnityScript. This game will include movement, collisions, triggers, states, projectiles, boundaries, and randomly spawning entities.

6

Game #1 – Roguelike

"The family of roguelike games is based on the video game Rogue, programmed for Unix-based systems in 1980."

– Jeremy Parish, The Essential 50 Part 12 – Rogue,
http://www.1up.com/features/essential-50-rogue

Overview

In this chapter, we will learn how to create our very first basic 2D game in Unity with UnityScript! This game will include movement, collisions, states, projectiles, and randomly spawning entities.

The following is the list of topics that will be covered in the chapter:

- What is Roguelike?
- Background
- Animating the hero
- Movement controls
- Randomly spawning enemies
- Animating the enemy
- Enemy movement
- Shooting projectiles
- Collisions
- Permadeath

What is Roguelike?

Roguelike is a genre of games that includes the following game elements: a fantasy theme, random levels, permadeath (permanent death), and tile-based graphics.

However, there are many variations that make the genre innovative using some of those elements at varying degrees together with elements that do not normally fall within the Roguelike genre.

There has been a huge boom in Roguelike games recently with many successful new indie Roguelike games being released.

The game design advantages they provide are as follows:

- **Replay value**: Players can play the game over and over again. Each game feels unique since it contains random elements.

- **Simplicity**: Roguelike games can be simple since they already provide enough variety with their randomness and challenge difficulty.

- **Accountability**: Players feel the need to be responsible for their actions and improve their strategy; otherwise, they will lose their character's progress permanently.

- **Challenging**: With permanent death, players really feel the challenge in difficulty.

The main game development advantage that they provide is that they are normally simple to create yet provide variety and challenge.

The following screenshot displays Nethack, a Roguelike game:

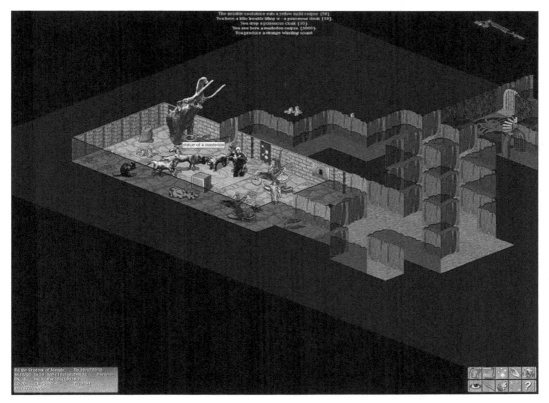

Nethack, viewed July 12, 2014, http://en.wikipedia.org/wiki/
Roguelike#mediaviewer/File:Vultures-2.1.0_screenshot.jpg

Adding a background

The first thing we need to do is create a new project by going to **File | New Project...** and name it Roguelike. We can then add a background to our game. We download and unzip the image Grassbg.png that we will use for our background from the following URL:

http://freeartsprites.com/roguelike/

We simply add the following sprite to our scene and resize it to cover the entire camera view:

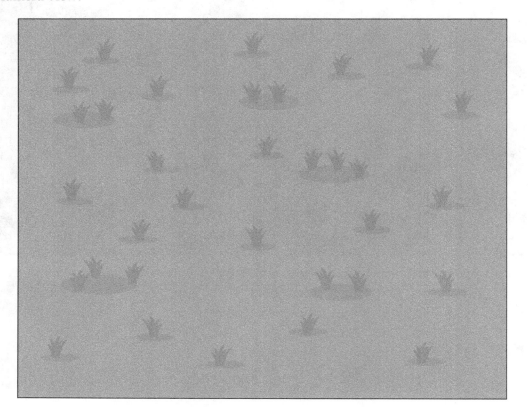

We name the sprite background. Then, we set the value of the **Order in Layer** option in **Sprite Renderer** to **-1**.

Animating the hero

The next thing we need to do is add a hero to the game. We will want to animate our hero as our hero is organic and not an inanimate object. We download and unzip the hero's sprite sheet `WizardSpriteSheet.png` from the following URL:

`http://freeartsprites.com/roguelike/`

The Wizard sprite sheet is shown in the following image:

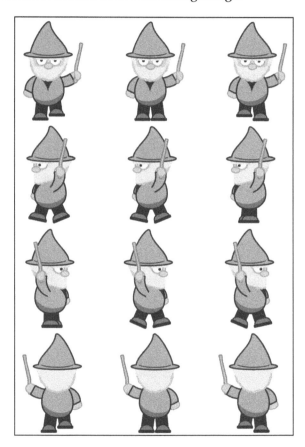

1. Slice the sprite sheet using the grid option, and use the dimensions **X** = 348, **Y** = 384, and **Pivot** = Center.

2. Create a hero GameObject. Name the GameObject `hero`.

3. Add a Box Collider by going to **Add Component | Physics 2D | Box Collider 2D**.

We now create the first animation of the hero walking down.

The Walking Down animation

We click on the hero and then open the Animation View by going to
Window | Animation.

1. Click on the empty space to open the drop-down menu, and then
   go to **Create New Clip** as shown in the following screenshot:

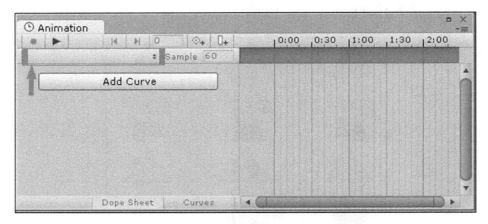

2. We name the animation `walkDown.anim`.
3. Set the **Sample** option to 5.
4. Add the following sprite `WizardSpriteSheet_0` at the frame location **0:00**
   on the animation timeline by simply dragging the sprite asset beneath **0:00**:

5. Add the following sprite WizardSpriteSheet_1 at the frame location **0:10** on the animation timeline by simply dragging the sprite asset beneath **0:10**:

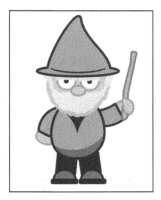

6. Add the following sprite WizardSpriteSheet_2 at the frame location **0:20** on the animation timeline by simply dragging the sprite asset beneath **0:20**:

7. Add the sprite WizardSpriteSheet_1 again at the frame location **0:30** on the animation timeline by simply dragging the sprite asset beneath **0:30**.

 Make sure that you stop recording by clicking on the record button so that it is no longer selected in a red tint.

8. We should have the result shown in the following screenshot:

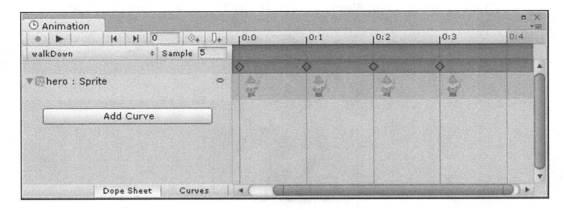

 If the sprites were in the correct order within the sprite sheet, then a quicker way of creating the animation is to select all the sprites for that animation and dragging them all at once onto the Animation View timeline and then setting the **Sample** option to 5 to space them out. This way, the animation does not play too fast, but instead at the speed of 5 frames per second.

The Walking Left animation

Following from the Walking Down animation, let's move to the left by executing the following steps:

1. Select **Create New Clip** from the drop-down menu.
2. Name the animation `walkLeft.anim`.
3. Set the **Sample** option to 5.
4. Set the timeline as per the following table:

Sprite Name	Timeline Frame
WizardSpriteSheet_3	0:00
WizardSpriteSheet_5	0:10
WizardSpriteSheet_4	0:20
WizardSpriteSheet_5	0:30

The Walking Right animation

Now, it's time to move to the right. Let's execute the following steps to do this:

1. Select **Create New Clip** from the drop-down menu.
2. Name the animation `walkRight.anim`.
3. Set the **Sample** option to 5.
4. Set the timeline as per the following table:

Sprite name	Timeline frame
WizardSpriteSheet_7	0:00
WizardSpriteSheet_6	0:10
WizardSpriteSheet_8	0:20
WizardSpriteSheet_6	0:30

The Walking Up animation

Let's finish the walking while moving upwards.

1. Select **Create New Clip** from the drop-down menu.
2. Name the animation `walkUp.anim`.
3. Set the **Sample** option to 5.
4. Set the timeline as per the following table:

Sprite name	Timeline frame
WizardSpriteSheet_9	0:00
WizardSpriteSheet_10	0:10
WizardSpriteSheet_11	0:20
WizardSpriteSheet_10	0:30

 We covered animation creation in *Chapter 3, Add Some Character*. Please refer to this chapter for more information.

Movement controls

Now that we have our hero character's animations ready, we can detect input from the player in order to control the hero's movement.

We will play the animation that corresponds with the direction that the hero is moving. We will use the *W*, *A*, *S*, and *D* keys on our keyboard as our movement keys.

Before we can detect input in script and then output the corresponding animation, we first need to set the states and order the transitions between multiple animations using the Animator.

Movement Controls Animator

We assign the Animator component to the hero GameObject within the Inspector by going to **Add Component | Miscellaneous | Animator**. Then, within the Animator View (you can open this by going to **Window | Animator**), order the animation states we created by right-clicking and adding transitions with directions that match the following screenshot:

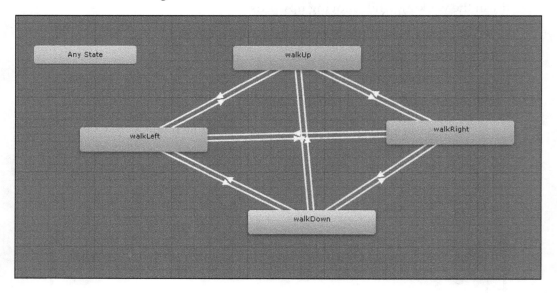

We add the following Boolean parameters to the **Parameters** box within the Animator View. To do this, we click on the plus sign, select **Bool**, and then name the parameters as follows:

- right
- down

- up
- left

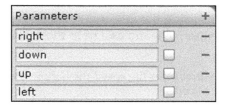

We click on each transition individually and check the Inspector. At the bottom of the Inspector, we set the condition to match the direction the transition arrow is pointing to, with the name of the corresponding parameter. For instance, if the arrow is going from `walkDown` and pointing towards `walkRight`, we select the right parameter. Similarly, if the transition is going from `walkLeft` to `walkRight`, we again select the right parameter. However, if the transition is going from `walkRight` to `walkLeft`, then we select the left parameter.

The following screenshot displays the location of the condition within the Inspector:

Movement controls script

We move the hero on the lines of the movement script we created in *Chapter 4, Code Control*. The main addition here is that we set the values of the parameters we have created within the Animator using the `animator.setBool` function in the following script, which we will name `Hero.js` and assign to the hero character:

 Declare the variable for the speed the hero will move at as shown in the next line of code.

```
var speed:float = 2.0;
```

 Declare the direction variables for the movement states that the hero will travel at on his own. This is shown in the next code snippet.

```
var right:boolean = false;
var left:boolean = false;
var up:boolean = false;
var down:boolean = false;
```

 Declare the variable to store the Animator component attached to the ninja GameObject.

```
var animator: Animator;
```

 At the start of our game, we get the Animator component attached to our ninja GameObject and assign it to our Animator variable we declared so that we can access the parameters within the Animator.

```
function Start()
{
animator = GetComponent("Animator");
}
```

 We call our `MoveCharacter` function within `Fixed Update` instead of `Update` as we are using a Rigidbody – when using **Physics**, we need to ensure that the updates occur in sync with the Physics engine as using `Update` could cause inconsistencies depending on the frame rate of the game.

```
function FixedUpdate()
{
MoveCharacter();
}
```

 There is a function to move the hero. This is shown in the next line of code.

```
function MoveCharacter()
{
```

 Detect if the input key from the keyboard is *D*. This is shown in the next line of code.

```
if (Input.GetKey(KeyCode.D))
{
```

 If the *D* key is pressed, then we call the Animator function and set the `right` parameter of the Animator's `bool` function to `true` and the rest of the parameters to `false`. This is so that the other animations transition to the `walkRight` animation. This is shown in the next code snippet.

```
animator.SetBool("left", false);
animator.SetBool("up", false);
animator.SetBool("down", false);
animator.SetBool("right", true);
```

 We do the same with the movement states. This is shown in the next code snippet.

```
down = false;
left = false;
right = true;
up = false;
```

 Move the character to the right using `transform.Translate`, which is the function that moves a GameObject's position based on direction and distance. The first parameter passes the direction, and the next two parameters, being speed and time, pass the distance as distance is speed over time.

We use `Vector3.right`, which is the shorthand for a predefined vector moving right which is (-1,0,0).

We then multiply by the speed that we want the character to move right at and then the amount of time we want the character to be moving right, which in this case is for as long as the player is pressing down the *D* key.

We use `Time.deltaTime` for this as it makes the movement frame independent, allowing the character to move a certain distance per second instead of per frame because it calculates the seconds that have passed since the last frame. This is shown in the next code snippet.

```
    transform.Translate(Vector3.right * speed * Time.deltaTime);
}
```

Once we have moved the hero to the right and therefore set his movement state to the right, he will continue moving to the right on his own when we are no longer pressing the *D* key. This is shown in the next code snippet.

```
if (right == true)
{
    transform.Translate(Vector3.right * speed * Time.deltaTime);
}
```

Once we have moved the hero to the left and therefore set his movement state to the left, he will continue moving to the left on his own when we are no longer pressing the *A* key. This is shown in the next code snippet.

```
if (left == true)
{
    transform.Translate(Vector3.left * speed * Time.deltaTime);
}
```

Once we have moved the hero up and therefore set his movement state to up, he will continue moving up on his own when we are no longer pressing the *W* key. This is shown in the next code snippet:

```
if (up == true)
{
  transform.Translate(Vector3.up * speed * Time.deltaTime);
}
```

 Once we have moved the hero down and therefore set his movement state to down, he will continue moving down on his own when we are no longer pressing the *S* key. This is shown in the next code snippet.

```
if (down == true)
{
  transform.Translate(Vector3.down * speed * Time.deltaTime);
}
```

 Detect if the input key from keyboard is *S*. This is shown in the next line of code.

```
if (Input.GetKey(KeyCode.S))
{
```

 If the *S* key is pressed, then we call the Animator function and set the the down parameter Animator's `bool` function to `true` and the rest of the parameters to `false`. This is so that the other animations transition to the `walkDown` animation.

```
  animator.SetBool("left", false);
  animator.SetBool("up", false);
  animator.SetBool("right", false);
  animator.SetBool("down", true);
```

 We do the same with the movement states. This is shown in the next code snippet.

```
  down = true;
  left = false;
  right = false;
  up = false;
```

The hero moves down while we are pressing the *S* key. This is shown in the next line of code.

```
transform.Translate(Vector3.down * speed * Time.deltaTime);
}
```

 Detect if the input key from the keyboard is *A*. This is shown in the next line of code.

```
if (Input.GetKey(KeyCode.A))
{
```

 If the *A* key is pressed, then we call the Animator function and set the `left` parameter of the Animator's `bool` function to `true` and the rest of the parameters to `false`. This is so that the other animations transition to the `walkLeft` animation. Have a look at the next lines of code.

```
animator.SetBool("down", false);
  animator.SetBool("right", false);
  animator.SetBool("up", false);
  animator.SetBool("left", true);
```

 We do the same with the movement states. Have a look at the next code snippet.

```
  down = false;
  left = true;
  right = false;
  up = false;
```

 The hero moves left while we are pressing the *A* key. Have a look at the next line of code.

```
  transform.Translate(Vector3.left * speed * Time.deltaTime);
}
```

Detect if the input key from the keyboard is *W*. Have a look at the next line of code.

```
if (Input.GetKey(KeyCode.W))
{
```

 If the *W* key is pressed, then we call the Animator function and set the up parameter Animator's `bool` function to `true` and the rest of the parameters to `false`. This is so that the other animations transition to the Walking Up animation. Have a look at the next code snippet.

```
animator.SetBool("right", false);
animator.SetBool("down", false);
animator.SetBool("left", false);
animator.SetBool("up", true);
```

 We do the same with the movement states. Have a look at the next code snippet.

```
down = false;
left = false;
right = false;
up = true;
```

 The hero moves up while we press the *W* key. Have a look at the next line of code.

```
transform.Translate(Vector3.up * speed * Time.deltaTime);
}
}
```

Randomly spawning enemies

We are now going to add enemies to the game. Let's do this by executing the following steps:

1. To add the enemy, we download and unzip the `DwarfSpriteSheet` file from the following URL:

   `http://freeartsprites.com/roguelike/`

   The Dwarf sprite sheet is shown in the following image:

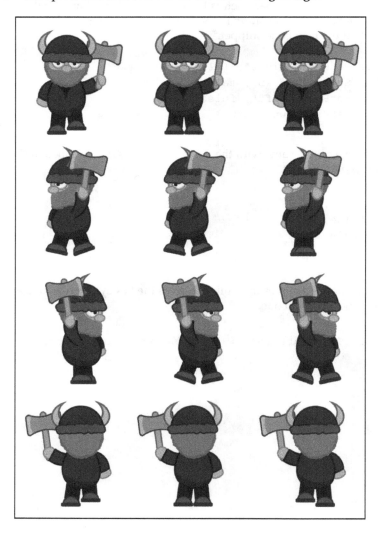

2. Slice the sprite sheet and create an enemy GameObject.

3. Name the GameObject `enemy`.

4. Add a Box Collider by going to **Add Component | Physics 2D | Box Collider 2D**.

5. Add a **Rigidbody 2D** component to our enemy GameObject by going to **Add Component | Physics 2D | Rigidbody 2D**.

6. Create the enemy idle animation the same way we created the hero idle animation.

7. We spawn multiple enemies by creating instances of our enemy GameObject.

8. Add the following lines to our hero script:

```
var enemy:Rigidbody2D;

function enemySpawn()
{
var enemyInstance:Rigidbody2D;


  enemyInstance = Instantiate(enemy,
    Vector3(Random.Range(2, 8),Random.Range(-4, 4),0),
    Quaternion.Euler(new Vector3(0,0,0)));
  }
```

9. Within the `start()` function's braces, we add the following line to call the function once at the very start of the game:

```
enemySpawn();
```

10. Finally, we add the following line of script within the hero script outside of any functions:

```
InvokeRepeating("enemySpawn", 3, 3);
```

This is a built-in Unity method that will repeatedly call the function at the times we set, starting at three seconds after the game has started and then every three seconds after that.

When the function is called, it will create an enemy at a random x and y location within the ranges that we set `Random.Range(2, 8)` and `Random.Range(-4, 4)` respectively.

The preceding script will not work unless we assign a value to the enemy variable within the Unity Editor.

Refer to the *Destroying the enemy* section in *Chapter 4, Code Control* on how to assign unassigned variables that we declare in the script within the Inspector in Unity.

Animating the enemy

Similar to the hero, we create four animations for all four directions that the enemy will travel in:

- enemyWalkLeft.anim
- enemyWalkRight.anim
- enemyWalkUp.anim
- enemyWalkDown.anim

We add the Animator component and set it up exactly the same way as we did for the hero.

Make sure to add the parameters just as we did for the hero and name them enemyLeft, enemyRight, enemyUp, and enemyDown.

Enemy movement

To move our enemies, we create a script similar to the hero's movement controls script. The only additions are the Accelerate and InvokeRepeating functions.

Accelerate increases the speed of the enemies' movement and InvokeRepeating calls the Accelerate function to increase the enemies' speed every five seconds.

The enemy will follow the movements of the hero moving diagonally to catch up with the hero and therefore have a more natural, realistic movement.

Add the following script, name it `enemy.js`, and assign it to our enemy GameObject:

```
var heroObj:GameObject;

var enemyRight:boolean = false;
var enemyLeft:boolean = false;
var enemyUp:boolean = false;
var enemyDown:boolean = false;
var enemySpeed:float;
var enemyAnimator: Animator;

InvokeRepeating("Accelerate", 2, 5);

function Start()
{
enemySpeed = 1.0;
}

function Update()
{
enemyMove();
}


function enemyMove()
{
```

 For performance and best practice, we could move the `Find()` method within the `Start()` function instead of being performed in every `Update()`. These are slow methods and Unity recommends that we avoid using them inside `Update()` unless necessary.

```
heroObj = GameObject.Find("hero");
enemyAnimator = GetComponent("Animator");
if (heroObj != null)
{
if (transform.position.y > heroObj.transform.position.y)
{
```

```
        enemyAnimator.SetBool("enemyLeft", false);
        enemyAnimator.SetBool("enemyUp", false);
        enemyAnimator.SetBool("enemyDown", true);
        enemyAnimator.SetBool("enemyRight", false);
        enemyDown = true;
        enemyLeft = false;
        enemyRight = false;
        enemyUp = false;
        transform.Translate(Vector3.down * enemySpeed *
            Time.deltaTime);

    }
    else
    {
        enemyAnimator.SetBool("enemyLeft", false);
        enemyAnimator.SetBool("enemyUp", true );
        enemyAnimator.SetBool("enemyDown", false );
        enemyAnimator.SetBool("enemyRight", false );
        enemyDown = false;
        enemyLeft = false;
        enemyRight = false;
        enemyUp = true;
        transform.Translate(Vector3.up * enemySpeed *
            Time.deltaTime);
    }

    if (transform.position.x < heroObj.transform.position.x)
    {

        enemyAnimator.SetBool("enemyLeft", false);
        enemyAnimator.SetBool("enemyUp", false );
        enemyAnimator.SetBool("enemyDown", false );
        enemyAnimator.SetBool("enemyRight", true );
        enemyDown = false;
        enemyLeft = false;
        enemyRight = true;
        enemyUp = false;
        transform.Translate(Vector3.right * enemySpeed *
            Time.deltaTime);
    }
    else
    {
```

```
        enemyAnimator.SetBool("enemyLeft", true);
        enemyAnimator.SetBool("enemyUp", false );
        enemyAnimator.SetBool("enemyDown", false );
        enemyAnimator.SetBool("enemyRight", false );
        enemyDown = false;
        enemyLeft = true;
        enemyRight = false;
        enemyUp = false;
        transform.Translate(Vector3.left * enemySpeed *
          Time.deltaTime);
    }
  }
}

function Accelerate()
{
enemySpeed = enemySpeed + 1;
}
```

Shooting projectiles

To ensure that the hero can fight and defeat the enemies, we will give him the ability to shoot magical orbs at the enemies. Let's execute the following steps to do this:

1. Create an orb GameObject by downloading and unzipping the Orb.png sprite from the following URL:

   http://freeartsprites.com/roguelike/

   The orb sprite is shown in the following image:

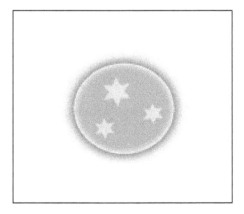

2. We name the orb GameObject `orb`.

3. Add a Circle Collider by going to **Add Component | Physics 2D | Circle Collider 2D**.

4. Then, go to **Add Component | Physics 2D | Rigidbody 2D**.

The script is similar to the previous shooting script that we created in *Chapter 4, Code Control*. The only difference is that we will add conditional checks to make sure that the hero can shoot in all four directions depending on which direction he is facing and traveling.

Add the following code to our hero script:

```
var orb:Rigidbody2D;
var orbSpeed:float = 20f;
var orbSpeed2:float = -20f;

function Update ()
{


var orbInstance:Rigidbody2D;


    if(Input.GetButtonDown("Fire1"))
    {


orbInstance = Instantiate(orb, transform.position,
  Quaternion.Euler(new Vector3(-1,0,0)));

if (right==true)
{
  orbInstance.velocity = new Vector2(orbSpeed, 0);
}
if (left==true)
{
  orbInstance.velocity = new Vector2(orbSpeed2, 0);
}


if (up==true)
{
```

```
      orbInstance.velocity = new Vector2(0, orbSpeed);
   }
if (down==true)
   {
      orbInstance.velocity = new Vector2(0, orbSpeed2);
   }

}
}
```

 The preceding script will not work unless we assign a value to the orb variable within the Unity Editor.

Refer to the *Destroying the enemy* section in *Chapter 4, Code Control*, on how to assign unassigned variables that we declare in a script within the Inspector in Unity.

Detecting collisions

In order to detect any collisions, we need to ensure that our hero, orb, and enemy GameObjects have **Box Collider 2D** components added to them.

When the magical orbs that we just added collide with an enemy, we want to destroy the enemy by detecting if the colliders of both the enemy and the orb collide.

Add the following code to the enemy script:

```
function OnCollisionEnter2D(other:Collision2D)
{
  if(other.gameObject.name=="orb(Clone)")
  {
    Destroy(other.gameObject);
    Destroy(gameObject);


  }

}
```

Permadeath

When an enemy collides with the hero, the hero will die, and the game will end. The point of the game is to try and survive for the longest time; therefore, the score is based on time.

We will use the OnGUI function to display the time counting up at the top-left corner of the screen. We will also check to see whether the hero collides with an enemy, and if so, then we destroy the hero and end the game.

Add the following script to the hero script:

```
#pragma strict

function OnGUI()
{

  GUI.Box (Rect (10,10,100,90), ""+Time.time);
}

function OnCollisionEnter2D(other:Collision2D){
  if((other.gameObject.name=="enemy(Clone)")||(
    other.gameObject.name=="right")||(other.gameObject.name==
    "left")||(other.gameObject.name=="bottom")||(
    other.gameObject.name=="top"))
  {
  Time.timeScale = 0;
  Destroy(gameObject);

  }

}
```

End game result

We can now press the play button in Unity to play our game. The following screenshot displays our Roguelike game:

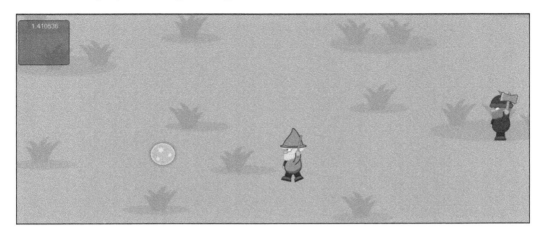

Summary

In this chapter, we created our very first 2D Roguelike game using Unity. The game consisted of a background, an animated hero that shoots projectiles, animated enemies that randomly spawn and follow the hero, and permadeath once a collision is detected. In the next chapter, we will learn about game conditions and how to display them on the screen by implementing a HUD with all the UI elements in a classic arcade game.

7

Game #2 – Classic Arcade

"To me the arcade experience is the ultimate gaming experience."

– Eugene Jarvis

Overview

In this chapter, we will learn about game conditions and how to display them on the screen. We will do this by implementing a HUD with all the UI elements into a classic arcade game. In brief, we will be looking at the following topics:

- Sponge antics
- Game conditions
- Lives
- Score
- Time
- Adding an HUD
- Font style
- The completed game

Sponge antics

For our second game, we will create a classic arcade game where the player will need to catch the falling *grime* while avoiding the falling cleaning acid.

Our main character – Spongy

Our main character is called Spongy, and it likes to keep the bathroom all sparkling clean. In order to do so, it must catch all the falling grime. However, Spongy must watch out for the falling cleaning chemicals as they contain acid that will harm it.

The bathroom

We will now create the environment of our game.

1. To begin with, we create our bathroom environment by adding the background to the scene from the following URL:

    ```
    http://freeartsprites.com/free-art/classic-arcade/
    ```

2. Name the background GameObject `Bathroom`.

    For this game, we will use the aspect ratio 5:4 (which is a screen resolution of 1280 x 1024 pixels) as the design of the game makes use of more height than width.

    This is because the game makes use of objects falling vertically from the top of the screen downwards.

3. To change our aspect ratio, we click on the drop-down box within the Game View, as shown in the following screenshot:

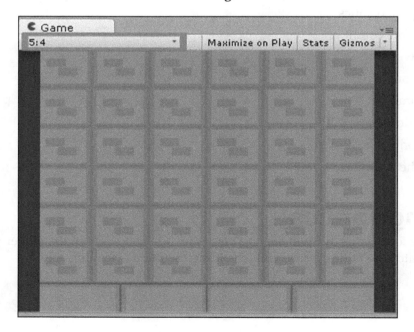

4. Move the background so that it fits perfectly in the scene. The background should fit perfectly since it has the exact same dimensions as the screen resolution we are using for this game.

Adding Spongy

We will now add our main character.

1. We now add Spongy using the `Sponge.png` file. To do this, we have to download `ClassicArcade.zip` from the following URL and unzip it:

   `http://freeartsprites.com/free-art/classic-arcade/`

2. Import the sprite into Unity.

3. We then slice the sprite sheet and use only one of the sprites, in a manner similar to the following image, as a GameObject:

4. Name this GameObject `Spongy`, and add the **Box Collider 2D** component by going to **Add Component | Physics 2D | Box Collider 2D** within the Inspector.

5. Move Spongy in the Scene View so that it is positioned above the bottom background tiles, as shown in the following screenshot:

6. Create a script called Spongy.js, and assign it to the Spongy GameObject.

Moving left and right

We now need to add the game controls for our game. To move Spongy left and right, we add the following script to the Spongy.js script:

 First, add a comment with the script name as shown in the next line of code.

```
//Spongy.js
```

 The next line of code is used to ensure strict typing—if you use the same variable for different data types, then an error will be thrown when building the script. This prevents bugs from occurring. Have a look at the next line of code.

```
#pragma strict
```

Declare a decimal variable and assign the 3 seconds speed that Spongy will move at. Have a look at the next line of code.

```
var speed:float = 3.0;
```

 The next line of code can be removed as it is not being used.

```
function Start ()
{

}
```

 The function to move Spongy gets called every frame. Have a look at the next code snippet.

```
function Update ()
{
  MoveCharacter();
}
```

 The next code snippet is a function to move Spongy.

```
function MoveCharacter()
{
```

 Detect whether the input key from the keyboard is *A*. This is shown in the next line of code.

```
if (Input.GetKey(KeyCode.A))
{
```

We then move Spongy using `transform.Translate`, which moves the transform in the direction and distance of the translation relative to something.

In this case, we translate Spongy's position using a 3D vector moving to the left direction multiplied by the distance of 3 units per second, which is speed multiplied by time moving relative to space since there is no third parameter.

We multiply against Delta Time to ensure that the animation is frame-rate independent; otherwise, should the frame rate drop at any time, the animation will slow down, and likewise, should it increase, the animation will speed up. Not only would this look wrong, but it would also not control correctly. The next line of code shows how this is done.

```
transform.Translate(Vector3.left * speed * Time.deltaTime);
}
```

Detect whether the input key from keyboard is *D*. The next line of code shows how this is done.

```
if (Input.GetKey(KeyCode.D))
{
```

We then move Spongy using `transform.Translate`, which moves the transform in the direction and distance of the translation relative to something.

In this case, we translate Spongy's position using a 3D vector moving to the right direction multiplied by the distance of 3 units per second, which is speed multiplied by time moving relative to space as there is no third parameter.

Spawning grime

We are now going to add the grime that will spawn from above and drop downwards towards Spongy. Let's execute the following steps to do this:

1. Add the grime by downloading the sprites from `http://freeartsprites.com/free-art/classic-arcade/`. We then slice the sprite sheet and use only one of the sprites as a GameObject, as shown in the following image:

2. We name this GameObject `Grime` and add the **Rigidbody 2D** component as well as the **Box Collider 2D** component.

3. We then create a script called `Grime.js` and assign it to the `Grime` GameObject.

4. To spawn the grime randomly, we add the following script to `Grime.js`:

 Add a comment with the script name. The next line of code shows how this is done.

```
//Grime.js
```

 The next line of code is used to ensure strict typing—if you use the same variable for different data types, then an error will be thrown when building the script. This prevents bugs from occurring. The next line of code shows how this is done.

```
#pragma strict
```

Declare our `grime` variable and set its data type to `Rigidbody2D`. Have a look at the next line of code.

```
var grime:Rigidbody2D;
```

 Declare a decimal variable and assign the 3 seconds speed that the grime will move at.

We set it to `-3` since we want it to move down. The next line of code shows how this is done.

```
var speed:float = -3.0;
```

 The next code can be removed as it is not being used by us.

```
function Start ()
{

}

function Update ()
{

}
```

 We use the `InvokeRepeating` function to spawn the grime by calling the `SpawnGrime` function with the first parameter.

The function is called starting at 3 seconds by the second parameter, and then it gets called repeatedly every 10 seconds specified by the third parameter. Have a look at the next line of code.

```
InvokeRepeating("SpawnGrime", 3, 10);
```

 The next function is used to spawn the grime.

```
function SpawnGrime()
{
```

Declare a variable of an instance of our `Rigidbody2D` GameObject. The next line of code shows how this is done.

```
var grimeInstance:Rigidbody2D;
```

 Spawn an instance of the obstacle GameObject using the Unity function `Instantiate` and assign it to our variable.

The first parameter is the `gameobject`. We want to make an instance of the grime.

The second parameter is the position of the newly spawned grime whereby we use a vector with a random range of coordinates between `-8` and `8` along the *x* axis, a *y* coordinate of `7`, and a *z* coordinate of `0` as this is a 2D game.

The final parameter is the rotation/orientation of the newly spawned grime, and thus we use a quaternion. Within it, we create a new 3D vector because the variable is uninitialized. Have a look at the next code snippet.

```
grimeInstance = Instantiate(grime, Vector3(Random.Range(-8,
    8),7,0), Quaternion.Euler(new Vector3(0,0,0)));
grimeInstance.name = "Grime(Clone)";
```

 Using the `velocity` variable with a speed parameter along the *y* axis of a 2D vector will make the object move by itself because the Unity physics engine will move it for us. This is fundamentally different from our manually moving an object using the `Translate()` method.

```
grimeInstance.velocity = new Vector2(0, speed);

}



function OnCollisionEnter2D(other:Collision2D)
{

    if(other.gameObject.name=="Spongy")
    {
        Destroy(gameObject);
    }

}
```

Each instance creates a new name for the respective occurrence, for example, `Grime(Clone)`, then `Grime(Clone)(Clone)`, `Grime(Clone)(Clone)(Clone)`, and so on. A way to check whether Spongy is colliding with any of them is to rename all of them to `Grime(Clone)`.

This is the reason we used the following line in the previous script right before the preceding code snippet:

```
grimeInstance.name = "Grime(Clone)";
```

We will use it for the acid as well. Make sure to assign the `grime` GameObject to the `grime` variable within the Inspector in the Unity Editor.

Spawning acid

Now, we will add the acid that will also fall from above in the following manner:

1. Add the acid sprite by downloading the given sprite from the following URL:

    `http://freeartsprites.com/free-art/classic-arcade/`

2. We then slice the sprite sheet and use only one of the sprites in the following image as a GameObject:

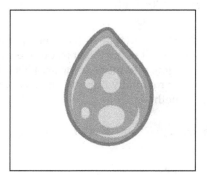

3. We name this GameObject `Acid` and add the **Rigidbody 2D** component as well as the **Box Collider 2D** component.

4. We then create a script called `Acid.js` and assign it to the `Acid` GameObject.

5. The script we will create is exactly the same as the script we created for the grime, the only difference being the naming of the script, function, and variables.

6. Add the following script to `Acid.js`:

```
//Acid.js

#pragma strict

var acid:Rigidbody2D;

var speed:float = -3.0;

var SpongyObj:GameObject;

function Start ()
{

}

function Update ()
{

}

InvokeRepeating("SpawnAcid", 3, 5);

function SpawnAcid()
{
  var acidInstance:Rigidbody2D;

acidInstance = Instantiate(acid, Vector3(Random.Range(-8,
  8),7,0), Quaternion.Euler(new Vector3(0,0,0)));
acidInstance.name = "Acid(Clone)";
acidInstance.velocity = new Vector2(0, speed);

}

function OnCollisionEnter2D(other:Collision2D)
{

    if(other.gameObject.name=="Spongy")
    {
        Destroy(gameObject);
    }

}
```

Make sure to assign the `Acid` GameObject to the `Acid.js` script within the Inspector in the Unity Editor.

Game conditions

Game conditions are the rules that dictate a victory or loss. This game will include the following conditions:

- Lives
- Timer
- Score

Lives

The player will start the game with three lives. Each time Spongy comes into contact with the acid blobs, the player will lose a life.

Should the player lose all three lives, then the game is over. To stop gameplay, we use the following line:

```
Time.timeScale = 0;
```

It is also useful for not only pausing and resuming, but also for slow and fast forward effects.

Add the following script to `Spongy.js`:

```
var lives:int = 3;


function OnCollisionEnter2D(other:Collision2D)
{
    if(other.gameObject.name=="Acid(Clone)")
    {
      lives = lives - 1;

    if (lives == 0)
    {
    Time.timeScale = 0;

    }

  }

  //will add score here

}
```

Score

The main objective of victory is the score. For each grime that Spongy collects, the player receives an added score of 50 points.

1. Add the following variable to `Spongy.js` at the very top:

    ```
    var score:int = 0;
    ```

2. Insert the following script beneath the comment `//will add score here`:

    ```
    if(other.gameObject.name=="Grime(Clone)")
        {
            score = score + 50;
        }
    ```

Time

The game will also include time as a secondary objective to show how long the player has survived each play. We will add our time using `Time.time` within the **heads-up display (HUD)** mentioned next.

Adding an HUD

To add the HUD that will display lives, score, and time, we add the following script to `Spongy.js`:

```
function OnGUI()
{
  GUI.Box (Rect (10,10,100,30), "Time: "+Time.time);
  GUI.Box (Rect (500,10,100,30), "Score: "+score);
  GUI.Box (Rect (600,10,100,30), "Lives: "+lives);
}
```

Using the existing Unity GUI function that gets called automatically, we create a rectangle with a size that we specify consisting of the *x* and *y* starting position of the rectangle followed by the *x* and *y* ending position.

We then add the string of text that we would like to display within the box followed by the plus sign and the variable. The plus sign concatenates (joins) the variable into the string so that it can be displayed as a string since the `GUI.Box` method can only display string types.

Font style

To edit the font that displays on our HUD, we add the following line of script to the Spongy.js script at the very top of the script alongside the other variables:

```
Var myStyle: GUIStyle;
```

When we click on the Spongy GameObject, we should get the following in the Inspector:

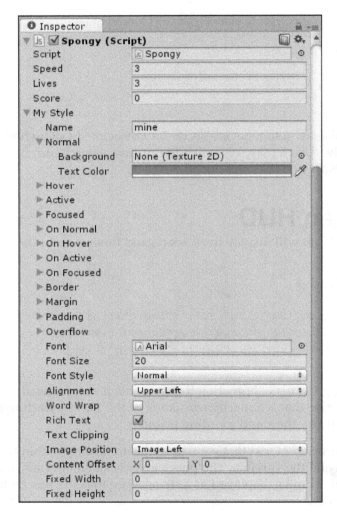

When clicking on the **My Style** drop-down list, there are many sub-attributes that we can edit in order to create our own font style. For instance, we can change the timer's color from black to red by going to **Normal** | **Text Color** and selecting red.

We can also make the font bigger by setting the **Font Size** option to 20.

To apply it to the timer so that the changes only affect the Timer HUD, we add myStyle to the existing timer GUI.Box that we have already created, as shown in the following script:

```
GUI.Box (Rect (10,10,100,30), "Time: "+Time.time, myStyle);
```

Resource management

When developing games, it is vital that we are wise at resource management and reuse the resources available to us. We should not waste resources since devices do not have an infinite amount of resources available.

Thus, by wasting resources, we are increasing the overhead on the device's memory and processor, impacting performance. For instance, if we keep creating many new objects in a scene, there is a huge amount of information to store, calculate, and handle. This will slow down the game and could potentially crash the game due to it running out of memory or an overload of calculations.

It is therefore best practice to reuse or destroy (remove) objects once they are no longer needed, particularly when they are no longer on screen.

Garbage collection is a type of memory management whereby the garbage collector tries to reclaim memory that is no longer being used by the game. Unity performs garbage collection automatically; however, based on the game's design, we need to decide when objects need to be created and destroyed.

In order to delete all the grime objects in the scene (both on screen and off screen) at the end of the game, we need to group the objects.

In Unity, we use tags to group objects.

To create a tag, we have to execute the following steps:

1. We select **Acid** in the hierarchy and then within the Inspector, we click on the **Tag** drop-down menu and select **Add Tag...**.
2. Within the **Element 0** field under **Tags & Layers**, we add Acid and within **Element 1**, we add **Grime**.
3. Select **Acid** from the hierarchy again and click on the **Tag** drop-down menu again; this time **Acid** will appear. Select **Acid**.

4. It should now look like what is shown in the following screenshot:

We do the same for `Grime`.

 As we want to keep track of all the objects, we need to place them in a list within the script. To achieve this, we will make use of an array since an array is a variable-sized list. Have a look at the next code snippet to learn how this is done.

```
var gameObjects : GameObject[];

function RemovalGrime()
{
```

 We check whether the GameObject is in the **Grime** tag group that we created.

```
    gameObjects =  GameObject.FindGameObjectsWithTag("Grime");
```

 We use a conditional `for` loop to go through each object stored in the list as many times as there are items in the list specified by the length of the GameObjects list (until the last item on the list) provided by the second parameter.

We start at the first item that is provided by the first parameter and increment by one each time to go on to the next object within the list. The next code snippet shows how this is done.

```
for(var i = 0 ; i < gameObjects.length ; i ++)
        Destroy(gameObjects[i]);
}
```

 We do the same for `Acid` as we did for `Grime`, merely swapping the names. Have a look at the next code snippet to learn how this is done.

```
function RemovalAcid()
{

    gameObjects =  GameObject.FindGameObjectsWithTag("Acid");

    for(var i = 0 ; i < gameObjects.length ; i ++)
        Destroy(gameObjects[i]);
}
```

We then need to make sure we call the new functions within the following part of existing script:

```
if (lives == 0)
    {
    RemovalAcid();
  RemovalGrime();
    Time.timeScale = 0;

    }
```

The completed game

By adding all the preceding GameObjects with their components into the scene and pressing play to test our game, we now have our completed game, which should look similar to what is shown in the following screenshot:

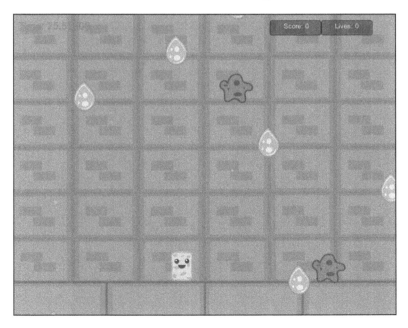

Summary

In this chapter, we learned about the widely used game conditions: lives, timer, and score, and how to display them on screen by implementing a HUD with all its elements in a classic arcade game. We also went into detail on how to set up our own font style.

In the next chapter, we will learn about the new 2D parallax scrolling in Unity and how to use it to create our own side-scrolling endless runner, polished up with particle effects.

8

Game #3 – Endless Runner

"The concept of an endless runner is simple. You run until you die. Despite its simplicity, endless running games are among the most ubiquitous and popular games in the App Store."

> *– Unknown author,* `http://appadvice.com/`
> `appguides/show/endless-running`

Overview

In this chapter, we will learn all about endless runners and about the new 2D parallax scrolling in Unity.

We will learn how to use the parallax scrolling to create our very own side-scrolling endless runner, polished up with particle effects:

- Infinite
- An agile ninja
- The ninja character
- Moving obstacles
- Survival
- Parallax scrolling
- Add pizzazz with particle effects
- Timer
- The result
- How to expand the game?

Infinite

Normally, a game follows a standard template with set rules. For instance, as their very basis, most games usually have a beginning and an end, which is similar to most other media, such as books, movies, and so on.

Mostly, this is due to the game following a story, however, even games that have no story still follow these rules as they provide a sense of completion and progression for the player.

There are even games that take this notion further by adding beats to the story with a climax and anticlimax providing the player with a sense of pace and allowing them to experience action-packed, adrenaline-pumping moments followed by slow-paced moments that allow them to rest.

And even still, there are other games that use foreshadowing moments to build up tension, which is very common in action, adventure, and horror games. However, the endless runner genre removes all that and allows players to play for as long as they would like, provided they survive that.

Since the game never truly ends, the player can enjoy the game over and over again. In order to create a game that has no beginning and ending, endless runners make use of random repetition to ensure that the game feels unique each time the player plays it.

The great advantage of this genre is that it provides an infinite amount of replay ability. Also, endless runners are far simpler and quicker to create; creating them is much simpler than creating bespoke levels.

With endless runners, we simply create the basic logic, and then the game will randomly create a unique experience with each play.

An agile ninja

For our third game, we will create an endless runner game about a ninja that is avoiding all obstacles using his agile skills of jumping and sliding.

The ninja character

Our ninja character needs to be an animated sprite that loops infinitely. The position of the ninja will remain static as we will move the background and foreground to give the illusion of movement.

To create our character, we execute the following steps:

1. Add a folder to **Assets** within the Project Browser named `Ninja`.
2. Download and unzip the image `NinjaSpriteSheet.png` from `http://freeartsprites.com/free-art/endless-runner/`.
3. Slice the sprite sheet into individual animation sprites.
4. Create a sprite GameObject using the following image:

5. Name the GameObject `Ninja`.
6. We then go to **Add component | Physics 2D | Box Collider 2D**.

Running

As we are creating an endless runner, we, of course, need our ninja to run! To create a run animation, we do the following:

1. Select the ninja from the hierarchy.
2. Go to **Window | Animation**.
3. Click on **Create New Clip**.
4. Save it as `Run.anim`.

5. Drag the following images into the timeline:

6. Set the sample to `10` to speed up the animation so that the ninja is running quickly.

Jump and Slide

Our ninja needs to be agile, and he, therefore, needs to be able to jump over and slide under any obstacle in his way.

To create his jump animation, we do the following:

1. Select the ninja from the hierarchy.
2. Go to **Window | Animation**.
3. Click on **Create New Clip**.
4. Save it as `Jump.anim`.
5. Drag the following images into the time frame:

6. Set the sample to 5 to slow down the jump animation.

To ensure that the ninja is not jumping on the same spot, we need to increase his height while he jumps. To achieve this, we go to **Add Curve** | **Transform** | **Position** and increase the y position by 1 unit on each frame for the first three frames. The following table will help us to get a clearer picture of this:

Frame	Position.y
0:0	-3
0:1	-2
0:2	-1
0:3	-2
0:4	-3
1:0	-3

To create this slide animation we do the following:

1. Select the ninja from the hierarchy.
2. Go to **Window** | **Animation**.
3. Click on **Create New Clip**.
4. Save it as `Slide.anim`.
5. Drag the following image into the time frame:

6. We can leave the sample at the default `60` as we are only using one key frame for the slide animation.

Add Animator parameters

We now need to add the Animator parameters by doing the following:

1. Go to **Window | Animator**.

2. We add the following Boolean parameters to the **Parameters** box within the Animator View by clicking on the **+** sign, selecting **Bool**, and then naming them as follows:

   ○   jump
   ○   slide

Ensure that both parameters are unchecked as they need to start as false by default, since the character will neither be jumping nor sliding but instead running by default.

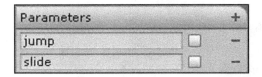

We will also add the run parameter in a similar way.

Animator states and transitions

Before we can detect a jump or slide in the script and then output the corresponding animation, we first need to set the states and order the transitions between the multiple animations by using the Animator. To do this, we can execute the following steps:

1. We assign the Animator component to the ninja GameObject within the Inspector. We generally do this by going to **Add Component | Miscellaneous | Animator**.

2. In the Inspector, within the Animator component, we set our controller. Click on **Controller** and select **Ninja**.

3. We now select the Animator View by going to **Window | Animator**.

4. In the Animator View, order the animation states that we created by right-clicking and adding transitions with directions that match the following screenshot:

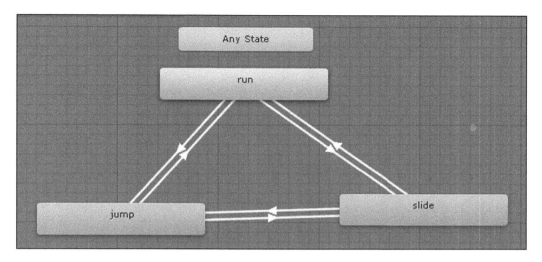

Ensure that **run** is set as default and is orange; if not, then right-click on it, and select **Set As Default**. We click on each transition individually and check the Inspector.

At the bottom of the Inspector, we set the condition to match the direction the transition arrow is pointing at, with the name of the corresponding parameter. The following are the conditions:

- If the arrow is going from **jump** and pointing towards **slide**, then we select the **slide** parameter

- Similarly, if the transition is going from **run** to **slide**, then we select the **slide** parameter

- However, if the transition is going from **slide** to **run**, then we select the **run** parameter

The following screenshot displays the location of the condition within the Inspector:

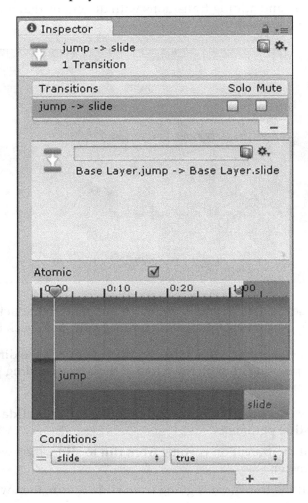

Movement controls

We are going to set up the movement controls that enable us to move the Ninja character. Now that we have set up the movement animations, we need to detect input in order to trigger each animation.

For our endless runner, we only need a jump control and a slide control.

We will use the *W* key to jump and the *S* key to slide.

To use these controls, we need to do the following:

1. Create a script and call it `Ninja.js`.

2. Assign the script to the **ninja** GameObject by going to **Add component | New Script**.

Within the script, we add the pieces of code following the information boxes:

This is used to ensure strict typing – if you use the same variable for different data types, then an error will be thrown when building the script. This prevents bugs from occurring. Have a look at the next line of code.

```
#pragma strict
```

Declare a variable to store the Animator component attached to the ninja GameObject. Have a look at the next line of code.

```
var animator: Animator;
```

At the start of our game, we get the Animator component attached to our ninja GameObject and assign it to our `animator` variable that we declared, so that we can access the parameters within the Animator.

```
function Start()
{
animator = GetComponent("Animator");
}
```

We call our `MoveCharacter` function within `FixedUpdate` instead of `Update` as we are using a rigid body – when using the Physics engine, we need to ensure that the updates occur in sync with the Physics engine as using `Update` could cause inconsistencies depending on the frame rate of the game. Also, the Physics engine updates rigid bodies at a fixed rate per second, whereas the rendering engine updates as many times as possible per second (or is limited to monitor the refresh rate). Have a look at the next code snippet.

```
function FixedUpdate ()
{
  MoveCharacter();
}
```

 The function to move the ninja is given next.

```
function MoveCharacter()
{
```

 Detect whether the input key from the keyboard is *W*. Next, you will see how this can be done.

```
if (Input.GetKey(KeyCode.W))
{
```

 If the *W* key is pressed, then we call the `animator` function and set the `jump` parameter of the Animator's `bool` function to `true` in order to trigger the jump transition so that the run animation or slide animation transitions to the jump animation. This can be done by adding the next code snippet.

```
    animator.SetBool("jump", true);
}
else
{
```

 If the *W* key is not pressed and, therefore, `false`, then the ninja should not jump, and we set the `jump` parameter of the Animator's `bool` function to `false`. Have a look at the following line of code.

```
animator.SetBool("jump", false);
}
```

 Detect whether the input key from the keyboard is *S*. Have a look at the next line of code.

```
if (Input.GetKey(KeyCode.S))
{
```

If true, then we call the `animator` function and set the `slide` parameter of the Animator's `bool` function to `true` to trigger the jump transition so that the run animation or jump animation transitions to the slide animation. Have a look at the next code snippet.

```
    animator.SetBool("slide", true);
}
else
{
```

 If the *S* key is not pressed and, therefore, false, then the ninja should not slide, and we set the `slide` parameter of the Animator's `bool` function to `false`. Have a look at the next code snippet.

```
    animator.SetBool("slide", false);
    }
}
```

Randomly repeating obstacles

We are going to create obstacles for the ninja to avoid. These obstacles need to repeat until the player dies, and they need to spawn randomly to provide challenges, variety, and replay ability.

Since the player is static, the obstacles need to move towards the player. To create our obstacle, we can execute the following steps:

1. Add a folder to `Assets` within the Project Browser named `Obstacle`.

2. Download and unzip the image `Boulder.png` from `http://freeartsprites.com/free-art/endless-runner/`.

3. Create a sprite GameObject using the following image:

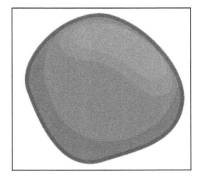

4. Position the boulder obstacle as in the following screenshot:

5. Name the GameObject `Obstacle`.
6. Go to **Add component** | **Physics 2D** | **Box2D Collider**.
7. Go to **Add component** | **Physics 2D** | **Rigidbody 2D**.
8. Set **Gravity** to `0`.
9. Create a script called `Obstacle.js`, and assign it to the `Obstacle` GameObject.

Add the following to the script:

 Declare our `obstacle` variable and set its data type to `Rigidbody2D`. This is shown in the next line of code.

```
var obstacle:Rigidbody2D;
```

 Declare a decimal variable and assign the 3 seconds speed that the ninja will move at. We set this to `-3` since we want it to move to the left-hand side. Have a look at the next line of code.

```
var speed:float = -3.0;
```

 Declare our `ninja` object of the type `GameObject`. You will see how this is done in the next line of code.

```
var ninjaObj:GameObject;
```

 We spawn an obstacle every 3 seconds using Unity's `Invoke` method. The first parameter we pass is the name of the function that spawns an obstacle and the second parameter is the delay in terms of seconds between each spawn. Have a look at the next line of code.

```
Invoke("SpawnObstacle", 3);
```

 The function to spawn an obstacle is given next.

```
function SpawnObstacle()
{
```

 Declare a variable of an instance of our `Rigidbody2D` GameObject.

```
var obstacleInstance:Rigidbody2D;
```

 Spawn an instance of the obstacle GameObject using Unity's `Instantiate` function and assign it to our variable. The first parameter is the GameObject we want to make an instance of, namely, the obstacle.

The second parameter is the position of the newly spawned obstacle, whereby we use a vector with three coordinates. The first coordinate *x* is set to 10; the second coordinate *y* uses a random range function to provide random height; and the final *z* position we leave at 0 as this is a 2D game.

The final parameter is the rotation/orientation of the newly spawned obstacle and thus we use a quaternion. Within it, we create a new 3D vector because the variable is uninitialized.

```
obstacleInstance = Instantiate(obstacle, Vector3(10,Random.Range(
    -4, 0),0), Quaternion.Euler(new Vector3(0,0,0)));
```

 We give all new instances identical names so that we can simply identify all of them; otherwise, we would have to check each individually. Have a look at the next line of code.

```
obstacleInstance.name = "Obstacle(Clone)";
```

 Set the obstacle instance's velocity in the *x* axis to the speed variable of -3.0 that we declared at the start of the script. We use a vector with two coordinates *x* and *y* for each position update. Have a look at the next line of code.

```
obstacleInstance.velocity = new Vector2(speed, 0);
}
```

Make sure to assign the obstacle Rigidbody to the `obstacle` variable under the script component in the Inspector.

Survival

In an endless runner, the character usually only has one life, and as such, we need to check our game. Check when the ninja collides with an obstacle, because when that happens, he dies and the game ends.

 A Unity function to detect whether the ninja has collided with an obstacle is declared next. We do not need to call the function since it is part of the Unity API and gets called automatically by Unity's Physics engine.

```
function OnCollisionEnter2D(other:Collision2D)
{
```

 If the name of the object that has collided with the obstacle is `Ninja`, then end the game by stopping the game using `Time.timeScale = 0;`. And then, destroy the obstacle. Have a look at the next code snippet.

```
    if(other.gameObject.name=="Ninja")
    {
        Time.timeScale = 0;
    Destroy(gameObject);
    }
}
```

Parallax scrolling

As we are creating an endless runner, we need our environment to seamlessly repeat infinitely. There are various ways to do this; however, with the new Unity 2D animation, we can simply use the 2D animation to accomplish this by animating the background moving.

To do so, we need to do the following:

1. Add a folder named `Background` to `Assets` within the Project Browser.

2. Download and unzip the `desert_BG.png` image from `http://freeartsprites.com/free-art/endless-runner/`.

3. Create a sprite GameObject using the following image:

4. Make a duplicate of the image by pressing *Crtl + D*, and position it on the right-hand side so that they are seamless.

5. Change the camera aspect ratio to 16:9.

6. Ensure that the left-hand side `desert_BG` object fits perfectly within the camera view.

7. Drag the right-hand side `desert_BG` object in the hierarchy onto the left-hand side `desert_BG` object so that the left-hand side object is the parent.

8. Now, select the left-hand side object, and open the Animation View:

9. Go to **Window** | **Animation**.

10. In the Animation View, create a new clip. Name it `ParallaxScrolling.anim`.

11. Go to **Add Curve** | **Transform** | **Position**. Set the sample to `2`.

12. Add a key on the very first frame of the timeline **0:0** and position the background relative to the camera, as shown in the following screenshot:

13. Now, add one more key on **5:0**, and move the left-hand side **desert_BG** object so that the right-hand side `desert_BG` object fits the scene perfectly, as shown in the following screenshot:

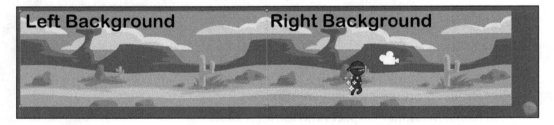

Add pizzazz with particle effects

Let's add some cool effects by simply adding dust to emphasize that the ninja is running and thus add more polish, realism, and immersion to our game.

To create our particle effect, we do the following:

1. Go to **GameObject | Create Other | Particle System**.

2. Position it by the ninja's feet.

3. Rotate it so that it faces the left-hand side since the dust will blow behind the ninja's feet. The following is the position of the ninja:

    X: 5

    Y: 270

    Z: 90

We will change the color so that it appears as sandy dust from the ground, as follows:

1. Select the particle system in the hierarchy.
2. Then, within the Inspector, click on the **Particle System** heading to open it. Now, click on **Start Color**, and change it to a light brown, as shown in the following screenshot:

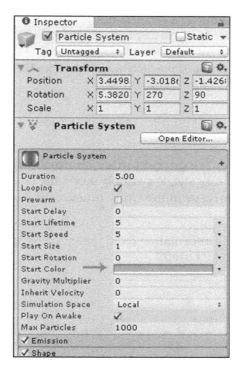

Displaying the timer

Commonly, in endless runners, other than distance and score, time is the main game condition and objective. Thus, we will display the time that the ninja has survived in a user interface at the top-left corner of the game.

Attach the following script to the end of the `Obstacle.js` script:

 Call the `OnGUI` function provided by Unity to create the GUI objects. The function is given next.

```
function OnGUI()
{
```

We use the GUI.box function to create the Timer GUI for our game using a rectangle. The first parameter we pass is the rectangle. We create the rectangle using four parameters within the rectangle function with the starting *x* and *y* coordinates for the top-left corner of the rectangle followed by the ending *x* and *y* coordinates at the bottom-right corner of the rectangle.

The next parameter we pass to the GUI.Box function is the Time: string we would like to display within our box, and we add the time value to our string so that it is also displayed.

Time.time returns the time in seconds since the game started. Have a look at the next line of code.

```
    GUI.Box (Rect (10,10,100,30), "Time: "+Time.time);
}
```

As with any Unity function, we can get further information from the Unity Scripting Reference on the official Unity site. We simply select the language that we are using from the drop-down menu, type in the Unity function that we are using, and do a search.

The following screenshot is information from the Unity Scripting Reference for the Gui.Box function we have just used:

GUI.Box

static function **Box(position**: Rect, **text**: string): void;
static function **Box(position**: Rect, **image**: Texture): void;
static function **Box(position**: Rect, **content**: GUIContent): void;
static function **Box(position**: Rect, **text**: string, **style**: GUIStyle): void;
static function **Box(position**: Rect, **image**: Texture, **style**: GUIStyle): void;
static function **Box(position**: Rect, **content**: GUIContent, **style**: GUIStyle): void;

Parameters

position	Rectangle on the screen to use for the box.
text	Text to display on the box.
image	Texture to display on the box.
content	Text, image and tooltip for this box.
style	The style to use. If left out, the box style from the current GUISkin is used.

Description

Make a graphical box.

```
    // Draws a box of the size of the screen.
    function OnGUI() {
            GUI.Box(Rect(0,0,Screen.width,Screen.height),"This is a title");
```

The result

We can now press play and test the agile ninja, our endless runner game. We should see the background scrolling, the dust particles emitting from behind the ninja's feet, and an obstacle randomly spawning repeatedly. To avoid the obstacles, we need to time the ninja's jump to go over obstacles and his slide to go under the obstacles.

We need to hold down the *W* key to perform a full jump, and likewise, we hold down the *S* key for as long as we want to slide.

It should look like what is shown in the following screenshot:

How to expand the game?

There is always room to expand a game. Try now to add more conditions or why not change the timer to display total distance. Add more varied obstacles or different shapes, sizes, and speeds. Add more varied effects and a start screen and a game-over screen.

We can always add more and more. What one has to keep in mind is not to overly complicate the game such that players get confused or frustrated. Also, time and resources can be limited, and the more you add, the more the platform will need to handle, and the more the bugs that can be introduced. The more we add, the more the game's release will be delayed, and if we never stop adding more content, mechanics, and features, our game may never ship!

This is why it is very important when first designing our game to ensure that we know what its main pillars are; otherwise, we could get ourselves into a situation that is known in the professional gaming industry as feature creep, whereby one keeps adding more and more.

Summary

In this chapter, we learned about the highly popular and successful endless runner genre of games and how to create our own endless runner using Unity's new parallax scrolling. We then polished it up with fanciful effects.

In the next chapter, we will learn about the new Box 2D Physics in Unity and how to use it to create a physics game similar to Angry Birds that simulates real-world physics.

Game #4 – Physics Fun

9

Overview

In this chapter, you will learn about the new 2D physics in Unity, including Box 2D physics and how to use it to create a physics game that simulates real-world physics, similar to Angry Birds.

The following list of topics will be covered in this chapter:

- The basics of physics
- Physics 2D
- Steps to create bodies
- What is Box2D?
- Let's simulate the world

The basics of physics

In order to make our games more realistic and therefore simulate real life, we make use of physics. However, to make use of it within our games, we first need to understand the basics of physics.

Just as a game needs rules in order to function, so too does the world around us. The natural world is governed by rules. The science that explains how the world is governed by these rules using measurable data is known as natural science. Physics is a branch of natural science that explains matter and the motion of matter through time and space.

Physics found in the real world

Physics covers an extremely vast range of concepts, and as such we will only look at the relevant basic quantities that provide the foundations of physics. The following are the basic quantities:

- **Matter**: Just as matter in the world is everything around us that is made up of atoms and molecules, in relation to games, the objects in our game are the matter in the game world.

- **Time**: We use time to set intervals on an object's movement or when we want events to be triggered, for example, when spawning an object.

- **Length**: This is a quantitative measurement of distance.

- **Vectors**: This is a quantity that has both direction and magnitude. A vector has x, y, and z coordinate values.

  We have been using vectors to position and move our objects.

- **Space**: This is an unoccupied area around us, and in the case of the game, our scene would be space.

- **Mass**: This is the amount of matter that an object is made up of.

- **Velocity**: This is the speed that something is moving at in a certain direction.

- **Acceleration**: This is the rate at which velocity changes at any given time.

- **Force**: This is the energy that results in movement.

- **Rigid body**: This is a solid body whereby deformation is neglected, so no matter how much force acts upon a rigid body, its form remains constantly rigid.

- **Drag**: This is the air or fluid resistance acting to slow down the velocity of an object.

- **Angular drag**: This is the same as drag, but it refers to the rotation of the resistance acting to slow down the rotational speed of an object.

- **Collision**: This occurs when multiple objects/bodies exert forces on each other for a certain amount of time.

- **Inertia**: This is the resistance of an object to move due to its mass. It is the desire for an object to stay moving at its current velocity, for instance, if moving to the left-hand side, keep moving to the left-hand side, or if at rest, keep staying at rest.

- **Momentum**: This is the product of the mass and velocity of a moving object/body.

- **Damping**: This is the resistance upon oscillations (to and fro motions like a spring moving). For instance, the higher the damping, the quicker a spring moving up and down will come to a stop, whereas the lower the damping, the longer it will take for a spring moving up and down to come to rest.

- **Gravity**: This is an object/body's force of attraction towards the center of the earth.

- **Friction**: This is the resistance that an object/body faces when moving over another object/body while in contact.

Physical quantities specific to physics engines (not in the real world) are as follows:

- **Kinematic**: This is the motion of an object/body without taking mass or forces into account.

- **Static**: This is the state of a non-moving object/body.

- **Interpolate**: This creates smoother movement by calculating the key data points between the start and end of the movement.

Physics 2D

Those of us that are already familiar with Unity are aware of the original Physics component. However, this component only works for 3D. There is now a new component specifically for 2D called Physics 2D. The Physics 2D Manager has the global settings for Physics 2D.

To access it, we do the following:

1. Go to **Edit** | **Project Settings** | **Physics 2D**. We would see the Physics 2D Manager as shown in the following screenshot:

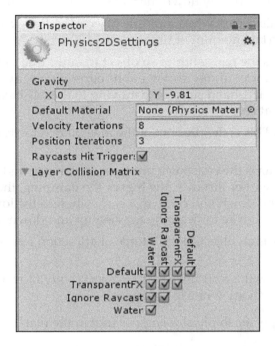

The Physics 2D Manager settings are as follows:

*   **Gravity**: We can set the global gravity that will affect all objects in our game. **X** is for horizontal gravity along the *x* axis and **Y** is for vertical gravity along the *y* axis.

*   **Default Material**: This is an assigned Physics 2D Material. By default, **None** is assigned.

*   **Velocity Iterations**: This is the number of iterations by the physics engine to calculate the changes in velocity of an object/body. The higher this value, the more accurate it is, but it is more expensive from the CPU's standpoint.

*   **Position Iterations**: This is the number of iterations by the physics engine to calculate the changes in position of an object/body. The higher this value, the more accurate it is, but it is more expensive from the CPU's standpoint.

*   **Raycast Hit Trigger**: If this option is ticked and therefore enabled, then whenever a collider is set as a trigger, a hit will be returned as true when it is hit by a raycast. If disabled, it will return false.

- **Layer Collision Matrix**: This sets which layers can interact with each other. By default, they are all enabled, so objects on any layer can collide with objects on any other layer.

A Physics 2D Material sets the friction and bounciness that occurs when multiple physics objects/bodies collide, as seen in the following screenshot:

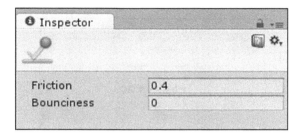

To create a Physics 2D Material, go to **Assets** | **Create** | **Physics Material 2D**.

What is Box2D?

The Physics 2D component makes use of Box2D. Box2D is a free, open source physics engine specifically designed for 2D by Erin Catto. It has been used in many successful 2D games, and is most widely known in the hit game Angry Birds.

To make use of the Physics 2D component, we go to **Add Component** | **Physics 2D**.

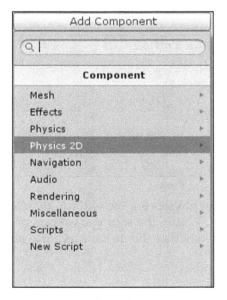

There are three collective types of Physics 2D components available:

- Rigidbodies
- Colliders
- Joints

The following screenshot displays them:

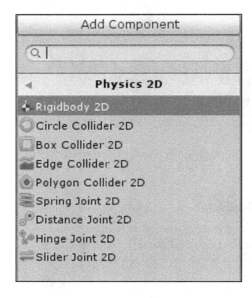

The following screenshot shows a collider:

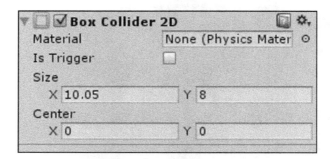

Colliders are shapes that the physics engine will use to determine collisions between the object and other objects. Within the settings, we can specify whether a collider uses a Physics 2D Material, whether this behave as a trigger or a collider, their size, and their offset.

The following screenshot shows a joint:

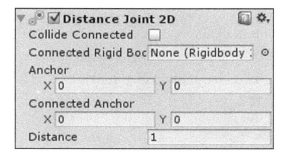

Joints join multiple objects together, for instance, a wall and a door, or the floor and a trapdoor, or even the arms of a robot. We can specify whether the joined objects can collide with each other, the object to join to, the anchor points, and the distance by which to separate the connected objects.

Steps to create bodies

The Rigidbody 2D component sets an object/body to be affected by physics. To create a Rigidbody, we can follow the same steps as our previous games by going to **Add Component | Physics 2D | Rigidbody 2D**.

The following screenshot shows the result:

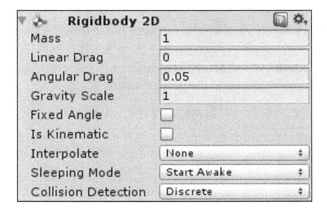

We will go through all the Rigidbody settings. These are described as follows:

- **Mass**: This refers to the mass of the object/body
- **Linear Drag**: This drag affects the movement in position
- **Angular Drag**: This drag affects the rotation of movement
- **Gravity Scale**: This is the amount of gravity that affects the object/body locally
- **Fixed Angle**: If this is enabled, then the Rigidbody is able to rotate when it's affected by a force
- **Is Kinematic**: This sets whether or not the Rigidbody is kinematic for instances where we want to manually animate the rigid body's position
- **Interpolate**: The interpolation settings between the physics engine's updates (when the physics calculations are updated)

Physics engines always have to run at a fixed frame rate regardless of the graphics frame rate. As these two frame rates generally don't line up, to render a game object with a rigid body, the renderer must interpolate or extrapolate based on two known times/ locations from the physics engine.

The following are the options under **Interpolate**:

- ° **None**: By default, **Interpolate** is set to none as it is only required when the movement of the Rigidbody is not smooth
- ° **Interpolate**: The object's movement is smoothed by taking into account the object's position from the previous frames
- ° **Extrapolate**: The object's movement is smoothed by estimating the object's position in the next frame

The following screenshot displays all the options:

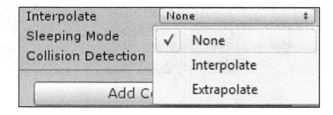

- **Sleeping Mode**: These settings are used to save processor time when the Rigidbody sleeps (rests).

The following are the options under **Sleeping Mode**:

- ° **Never Sleep**: This option is used to ensure the object never sleeps.
- ° **Start Awake**: When this option is used, the object is initially set to be awake and can then be set to sleep.
- ° **Start Asleep**: When this option is used, the object is initially set to sleep; however, it can be awoken by collisions.

The following screenshot displays all the options:

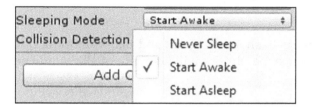

- **Collision Detection**: This consists of settings to detect collisions between the Rigidbody and other objects/bodies. The following are the options under this:

  - ° **Discrete**: A collision is detected if the object's collider collides with another collider during a physics update.

  - ° **Continuous**: Each physics update will perform extra work to make sure collisions are not missed. This is an important setting to use if we have very fast-moving rigid bodies. Fast-moving rigid bodies can miss colliding with each other if we use only the Discrete mode, but will not miss each other if we use the Continuous mode.

The following screenshot displays all the options:

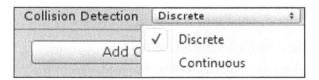

Let's simulate the world

Now that we have a better understanding of the basics of physics and we know about the new Physics 2D in Unity as well as Box2D, we are ready to make use of all these faculties to create our very own physics game.

We will create a very simple physics game similar to Angry Birds. We will have a cannon that shoots out cannonballs.

We can shoot out cannonballs by pressing the Space bar, and we can control where the ball lands by increasing or decreasing the power of the cannonball using the *W* and *S* keys.

The aim of the game is to shoot the crates and planks in the scene. We won't need to set up animations since the physics will take care of all the movements in the game.

The environment

The first thing we will do is create our scene with the background, foreground, and props that populate our environment.

Creating the scene

To create the scene, we do the following:

1. To create a new scene, go to **File | New Scene**.
2. Name it Scene and make sure you save it.
3. Within the Project Browser, under **Assets**, create a folder and name it Scenes.
4. Move the scene into the folder.

Creating the background

To create our background, we do the following:

1. Under **Assets**, create a folder and name it Background.
2. Add PhysicsBG.png as a sprite into the folder from the Chapter09_art bundle folder in the Code&ColoredImages bundle included with the book.

3. Create a sprite GameObject using the following image:

4. Rename it to `Background` in the hierarchy.
5. Position the background so that it fits perfectly in the Camera View.

The foreground

Our environment is also going to need foreground flooring so that all our objects can be placed in the scene; if we add our objects without a floor, then they will fall out of the scene.

This would not occur if we used static objects for our game or if we used physics with zero gravity. However, we are using objects that make use of physics as this is a physics game and we are simulating the world with the laws of gravity.

To create our foreground, we do the following:

1. Under **Assets**, create a folder and name it `Foreground`.
2. Add `PhysicsFloor.png` as a sprite into the folder, from the `Chapter09_art bundle` folder in the `Code&ColoredImages` bundle included with the book.
3. Create a sprite GameObject using the following image:

4. Rename it to Foreground in the hierarchy.

5. Position Foreground so that it fits perfectly in the Camera View at the very bottom.

6. Go to **Add Component | Physics 2D | Box Collider 2D**.

This will ensure the objects in our game collide with the ground when they fall.

Adding the props

We will add props in our screen, such as crates and planks, which will provide the targets for the cannonballs to collide with.

Adding the crate

To add the crate to our scene, we perform the following steps:

1. Under **Assets**, create a folder and name it Props.

2. Add Crate.png as a sprite into the folder, from the Chapter09_art bundle folder in the Code&ColoredImages bundle included with the book.

3. Create a sprite GameObject using the following image:

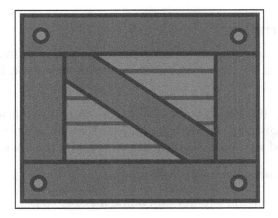

4. Rename it to Crate in the hierarchy.

5. Go to **Add Component | Physics 2D | Box Collider 2D**.

6. Go to **Add Component | Physics 2D | Rigidbody 2D**.

7. Create a few duplicates by pressing *Ctrl + D*. We can position them as we want.

Adding the plank

To add a plank to our scene, we do the following:

1. Click on the **Props** folder.
2. Add `Plank.png` as a sprite into the folder from the `Chapter09_art` bundle folder in the `Code&ColoredImages` bundle included with the book.
3. Create a sprite GameObject using the following image:

4. Rename it to `Plank` in the hierarchy.
5. Create a few duplicates.

   We can position them however we want.

6. Go to **Add Component | Physics 2D | Box Collider 2D**.
7. Go to **Add Component | Physics 2D | Rigidbody 2D**.

Shooting the cannonballs

We need a cannon that will shoot out cannonballs. To create our cannon, we need to do the following:

1. Add a folder to **Assets** within the Project Browser, and name it `Sprites`.
2. Add the `Cannon.png` sprite from the `Chapter09_art` bundle folder in the `Code&ColoredImages` bundle included with the book.
3. Create a sprite GameObject using the following image:

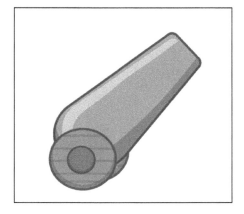

4. Name the GameObject `Cannon`.

5. Go to **Add Component | New Script** and name it `Cannon.js`.

6. Assign the script to the cannon.

7. In the Project Browser, add a folder named `Scripts` and move `Cannon.js` into it.

8. Add the following code to the script:

> The first line of code is used to ensure strict typing—if you use the same variable for different data types then an error will be thrown when building the script.
>
> This prevents bugs from occurring.

```
#pragma strict
```

> Declare our `cannonball` variable, and set its data type to `Rigidbody2D` as shown in the next line of code.

```
var cannonball:Rigidbody2D;
```

> Declare our `power` variable, set it to a decimal type, and assign it an initial default value of `30.0` that it will start with.
>
> We may need to adjust this value depending on our scene. Have a look at the next line of code.

```
var power:float = 30.0;
```

> Call the `OnGUI` function provided by Unity to create GUI objects.

```
function OnGUI()
{
```

We use the GUI.box function to create the Power GUI for our game using a rectangle. The first parameter we pass is the rectangle:

We create the rectangle using four parameters within the rectangle function with the starting (*x*, *y*) coordinates for the top-left corner of the rectangle followed by the ending bottom-right corner (*x*, *y*) coordinates of the rectangle.

The next parameter we pass to the GUI.Box function is the "Power:" string we would like to display as output feedback within our box, and we add the power value to our string so that it is also displayed.

```
    GUI.Box (Rect (10,10,100,30), "Power: "+power);
}
```

 We call our Cannonballs function within FixedUpdate instead of Update as we are using a Rigidbody. When using physics, we need to ensure that the updates occur in sync with the physics engine as using Update could cause inconsistencies depending on the frame rate of the game.

```
function FixedUpdate()
{

  Cannonballs();
}

function Cannonballs()
{
```

 Detect whether the input key from keyboard is *W*.

```
    if (Input.GetKey(KeyCode.W))
    {
```

We want to limit the power between 40 and 20 because if the power is too low, then the ball will not be able to blast out of the cannon, and if the power is too high, then the ball will go off screen.

Here, we limit the upper boundary of 40, so we only increase the power incrementally by 1 when pressing the *W* key if the power is less than or equal to 39. This is shown in the next code snippet.

```
if (power <= 39)
{

    power = power + 1;
}
}
```

Detect whether the input key from the keyboard is *S*. This can be done as shown in the next line of code.

```
if (Input.GetKey(KeyCode.S))
{
```

Here, we limit the lower boundary to 20, so we only decrease the power incrementally by 1 when pressing the *S* key if the power is more than or equal to 21. This can be done as shown in the next code snippet.

```
if (power >= 21)
{

    power = power - 1;
}
}
```

Detect whether the input key from the keyboard is the Space bar, and if it is, then we call the function that spawns cannonballs. This is shown in the next line of code.

```
    if (Input.GetKeyDown("space"))
    {

        SpawnCannonballs();
    }

}
```

 The function to spawn cannonballs from the cannon is shown next.

```
function SpawnCannonballs()
{
```

 To spawn cannonballs from the cannon when pressing Space bar in the game, we create an instance of our cannonball GameObject in the scene.

As our cannonball GameObject that we assign to our instance is a Rigidbody 2D (we have done so to abide by the laws of physics), we use the Rigidbody 2D data type.

```
var cannonballInstance:Rigidbody2D;
```

 We use Unity's Instantiate() function to create an instance of the cannonball Rigidbody 2D GameObject in our scene, and assign it to our cannonballInstance variable.

The first parameter is the cannonball GameObject, the second parameter is the position we want the instance to spawn, in this case, the *xyz* position of our cannon, and the third parameter is the rotation of the instance that we spawn.

```
cannonballInstance = Instantiate(cannonball, Vector3(
    -84,-40,72), Quaternion.Euler(new Vector3(0,0,0)));
```

 We need to make sure that we either position our cannon at the preceding coordinates (-84,-40,72) or, if our coordinates are different, then use the *x*, *y*, *z* positions of our cannon's position.

We rotate the cannonball instance's *z* rotation so that it looks right when it spawns and shoots out at the correct angle from the cannon. The *z* axis is the axis that points out from the screen towards you.

```
cannonballInstance.transform.Rotate(0,0,54);
```

> As pretty much all the physics has been simplified and is taken care for us with the Physics 2D component and the Box2D engine, we need only set the velocity of the `cannonballInstance` variable. We want the ball to travel up and to the right-hand side equally, and then with the cannonball's mass and the gravity pulling it down, we get the ball moving at a curve. This is shown in the next line of code.

```
cannonballInstance.velocity = new Vector2(power,power);
}
```

9. Build the script.

Creating the cannonballs

Now what fun is a cannon without any cannonballs? We now need to create the cannonballs that will shoot out of our cannon.

To create our cannonball, we need to do the following:

1. Within the `Sprites` folder, add the `Cannonball.png` sprite from the `Chapter09_art` bundle folder in the `Code&ColoredImages` bundle included with the book.

2. Create a sprite GameObject using the following image:

3. Name the GameObject `Cannonball`.
4. Go to **Add Component | Physics 2D | Circle Collider 2D**.
5. Go to **Add Component | Physics 2D | Rigidbody 2D**.

6. Select the cannon in the hierarchy, and within the cannon script in the Inspector, add the Cannonball Rigidbody 2D to the `Cannonball` variable.

We need to make sure that all the GameObjects in the scene are the same *z* distance from the camera as shown in the following screenshot:

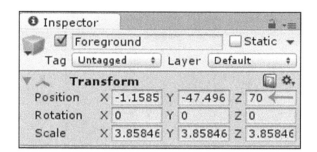

The final result

The final layout for the Project Browser should look like the following screenshot:

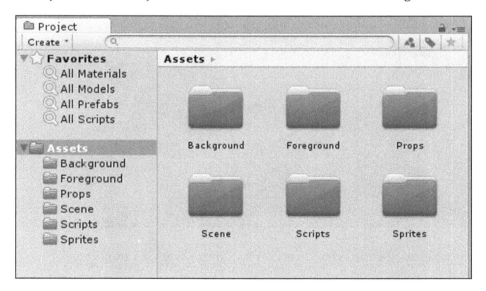

The final hierarchy should look like the following screenshot:

We can now try out our game. When we push play, we should see the following in the Game View:

The following zoomed in screenshot displays the power GUI output feedback:

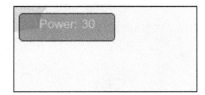

This value updates in real time when we press the *W* and *S* keys.

How do we extend it?

Using the collision script that we are familiar with, having used it in the prior games, try adding collectible objects among the crates or even destructible crates.

The cannonball can also be set up so that its rotation is controlled by the player. Try adding more physical quantities, such as acceleration and deceleration, more objectives, GUI, and feedback to the game.

Summary

In this chapter, you learned about the basics of physics and how to use physics in our own game using Unity's new Physics 2D, including the Box2D physics with bodies to simulate the real world.

In the final chapter, you will learn about audio, feedback, and deploying our game. You will put everything you have learned throughout the book into practice to create a game similar to Doodle Jump.

You will then be guided on your onward journey in 2D game development with a selection of useful resources.

10

You Are Ready!

"If you have a positive attitude and constantly strive to give your best effort, eventually you will overcome your immediate problems and find you are ready for greater challenges."

– Pat Riley

```
http://www.brainyquote.com/quotes/quotes/p/
patriley147924.html
```

Overview

In this final chapter, we will learn about audio, feedback, and deploying our game. We will combine everything that we have learned throughout the book to create a game similar to Doodle Jump. We will then be guided on our onward journey in 2D game development with a selection of useful resources.

Here's the list of topics that will be covered in the chapter:

- Audio
- Music
- Sound effects
- Saving and loading
- Triggers
- Cameras
- Multiplayer
- Putting it all together
- Deployment

- Your journey ahead
- A plethora of resources

Audio

To really bring our games to life, we normally need to add audio. Audio includes the following:

- Music
- Sound effects

Music

Music is not always necessary within a game; however, it can really make a game feel so much more atmospheric and exciting. Pacing the music successfully, one can add relaxing moments, foreboding moments, and tense, action-packed, climactic moments.

It can aid in the storytelling and expressionism or provide a unique form of escapism.

Sound effects

Sound effects add extra depth to a game and can be categorized as follows:

- **Ambient sound effects**: This comprises the surrounding environmental sound effects coming from all around.
- **GUI sound effects**: This comprises interface sound effects, consisting of clicks, button presses, and the like, providing feedback to the player.
- **Feedback sound effects output**: This comprises sound effects based on everything happening within the game, for instance, the character jumping, or when a player loses or wins in a level. All these sounds provide important feedback to the player allowing them to understand what is going on within the game to learn and improve or simply enjoy.

Saving and loading

As a player progresses through our games, we need to be able to store their progress values, whether they are their score, current level, health, ammunition, and so forth:

1. To save this data, we make use of the Unity function `PlayerPrefs`.

2. To store data, we use `PlayerPrefs.Set` followed by the data type we are using to store data. So, `PlayerPrefs.SetInt` is the function for an integer.

3. We then provide the reference name of the value we are storing followed by the actual variable that we would like to store. The following line of code is an example:

   ```
   PlayerPrefs.SetInt("level", level);
   ```

4. To retrieve and, therefore, load the stored data, we make use of `PlayerPrefs.Get` followed by the data type that we are loading, then the reference name, and lastly, we specify a value to assign should no existing data be saved.

   Thus, to load the level data, we use the following line of code:

   ```
   PlayerPrefs.GetInt("level", 1);
   ```

   Adding the second parameter is known as exception handling, whereby we respond to an occurrence because if we do not, then bugs or crashes could occur as a result.

   We simply catch potential errors that could occur and handle them.

5. Since the function is returning the stored value, we must ensure that we assign it to a variable such as the following:

   ```
   level = PlayerPrefs.GetInt("level", 1);
   ```

Creating a trigger

In all the previous games, we have made use of collisions; however, colliders can be set up as triggers that are very useful to trigger events. Similar to a collision, should one GameObject enter the trigger's area, then the script can be set up to trigger events on a successful overlap.

Thus, to create a trigger, we go to **Add Component | Physics 2D | Box Collider 2D** and then tick the **Is Trigger** setting.

The collider is no longer a collision, but now a trigger. In the script, we now replace the `OnCollisionEnter2D` function that we have been using with the trigger equivalent, that is, the `OnTriggerEnter2D` function.

Cameras

We have been using the Main Camera that is included by default within a new scene in Unity. We have kept it stationary since the games that we created had no need for a moving camera. However, most games will require camera movement, which will include panning, rotating, zooming, camera cuts, and so forth.

As with any GameObject in our scene, we can move a camera in the same manner using `transform.Translate`, as in the following script:

```
cam.transform.Translate(Vector3.up * camSpeed * Time.deltaTime);
```

For camera cuts or switching between cameras, we create multiple cameras by going to **GameObject | Create Other | Camera** and using the enabled property of the Camera component `cameraName.enabled`, as in the following script:

```
var cam1 : Camera;
var cam2 : Camera;

function Update()
{
if (Input.GetKeyDown("A"))
{
  cam1.enabled = true;
  cam2.enabled = false;
}
if (Input.GetKeyDown("D"))
{
  cam1.enabled = false;
  cam2.enabled = true;
}
}
```

Multiplayer

To add an online multiplayer would involve using networking, which is an advanced topic that requires an entire book to clearly explain everything that is required.

However, we can add a local multiplayer to our games, allowing more than one person to play together on the same device in the same location.

There are multiple ways of doing this:

- Pass and play
- Real time

Pass and play is very simple because the game functions as a single-player experience. The only difference is that we would need multiple separate profiles or sets of variables to store each player's data.

Real time is slightly more complex, requiring us to create multiple GameObjects in the scene to serve as the characters for each player. There is also the separate set of data for each player and each player's own separate and specific game controls. For instance, we can use the *WASD* keys for player 1 and the arrow keys for player 2, and so on.

Putting it all together

For our final game, we will take what we have learned from previous chapters and combine it with the concepts that we have just learned in this chapter to create a game similar to Doodle Jump. We will then see how to deploy our game. The following is the entire activity:

- We will create a platform game called *Space Buddy*
- Space Buddy is also the name of our main character, who is an alien
- Our alien, Space Buddy, will be jumping around the galaxy from one space platform to another trying to reach the top
- As he jumps around space, lava will rise from the bottom
- In this galaxy, gravity exists similar to our planet Earth, and should Space Buddy miss a platform, he will fall to his death into the lava, and the game will end
- However, his objective is to reach the UFO beam at the top of the level so that he can be transported to another galaxy
- Should he reach the beam successfully, then he will complete the first level successfully and go on to the next level
- Each time Space Buddy jumps, he increases his score by 50 points, and this score is carried over to the next level
- This game will make use of two levels, although it can be easily extended to include as many levels as we like

The first scene

To create the first scene, we do the following:

1. To create a new scene, go to **File | New Scene**.
2. Name it Scene.
3. Within the Project Browser, under **Assets**, create a folder and name it Scenes.
4. Move the scene into the folder.

The galaxy

To set the scene for our game, we need to add the galaxy background.

To add the background, we will execute the following steps:

1. Add a folder to **Assets** within the Project Browser and name it Background.
2. Download the image galaxy.png from the following URL:

   http://freeartsprites.com/platformer

3. Create a sprite GameObject using the following image:

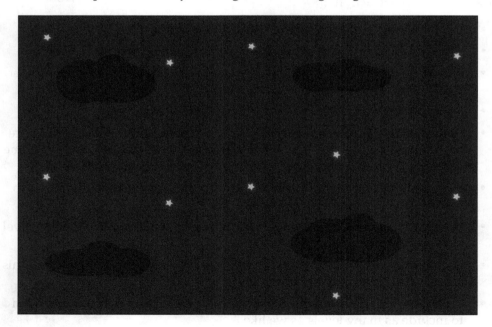

4. Name the GameObject Background.
5. Position it so that it covers the entire screen.

Platforms

We need to add platform props for Space Buddy to jump on so that he can reach the UFO beam that will be waiting above.

To add a platform, let's execute the following steps:

1. Add a folder to **Assets** within the Project Browser and name it `Props`.

2. Download the image `platform.png` from the following URL:

    `http://freeartsprites.com/platformer`

3. Create a sprite GameObject using the following image:

4. Name the GameObject `Platform`.

5. Duplicate it three more times to populate the scene.

Triggers

Instead of adding collision to our platform GameObjects as we normally did in the previous games, we need to make our platform triggers. This is because if we had them as collisions, then Space Buddy would not be able to pass through them and jump on them, but instead would collide with some of the platforms above him when jumping.

Thus, making them triggers instead allows Space Buddy to pass through and jump on them. To add triggers to the platforms, we execute the following steps:

1. Select a platform.

2. In the Inspector, go to **Add Component | Physics 2D | Box Collider 2D**.

3. Tick the checkbox next to the **Is Trigger** setting, as shown in the following screenshot:

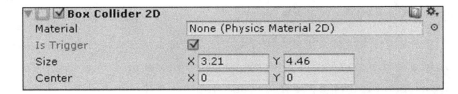

4. Make sure to do this for all the platforms.

The lava

The lava rises every time Space Buddy jumps. The game ends when Space Buddy falls into it.

To create the lava, let's execute the following steps:

1. Add a folder to **Assets** within the Project Browser and name it Foreground.

2. Download the image lava.png from the following URL:

   http://freeartsprites.com/platformer

3. Create a sprite GameObject using the following image:

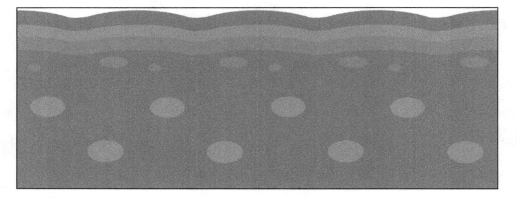

4. Name the GameObject Lava.

5. We add a trigger component to the Lava to check when the main character passes through to trigger the lose script that will destroy the main character. Go to **Add Component | Physics 2D | Box Collider 2D** and tick the **Is Trigger** setting.

UFO beam

The UFO beam is the main objective of each level. To successfully complete a level, Space Buddy needs to reach the UFO beam.

To create the UFO beam, let's execute the following steps:

1. Add a folder to **Assets** within the Project Browser and name it `Sprites`.

2. Download the image `UFObeam.png` from the following URL:

    `http://freeartsprites.com/platformer`

3. Create a sprite GameObject using the following image:

4. Name the GameObject `UFO beam`.

Adding audio

For the first time, we will be adding audio to our game. We will add sound effects for Space Buddy's jumps that will play each time he jumps on a platform as well as a sound effect when he dies and when he enters the UFO beam successfully, completing the level.

To add the sound effects, let's execute the following steps:

1. Add a folder to **Assets** within the Project Browser and name it `Audio`.

2. Download the audio wave file `spin_jump.wav` from the following URL:

    `http://soundbible.com/1898-Spin-Jump.html`

3. Drag the audio file into the Audio folder.

4. If we click on the imported audio asset file, we can select whether it is a 3D sound (sound manipulated to appear as if it is originating within a specific point in 3D space) or not, as well as its compression settings and therefore file size. When creating games for mobile platforms for instance, we need to keep files compressed and small in size. This does have a minimal effect on the audio quality. For a few very short sound effects, native (uncompressed) audio files can be used; they will not need to be decoded during runtime, thereby reducing runtime processing.

5. We repeat the preceding steps for jingles_NES00.ogg and jingles_NES01.ogg from SFX Jingles at the following URL:

    http://freeartsprites.com/audio

6. The following screenshot displays the audio formats supported by Unity:

Supported Formats

Format	Compressed as (Mac/PC)	Compressed as (Mobile)
MPEG(1/2/3)	Ogg Vorbis	MP3
Ogg Vorbis	Ogg Vorbis	MP3
WAV	Ogg Vorbis	MP3
AIFF	Ogg Vorbis	MP3
MOD	-	-
IT	-	-
S3M	-	-
XM	-	-

The camera

In this game, we want to ensure that Space Buddy is always on screen and that we can always see slightly ahead and below to assist gameplay. Thus, we will need to move our camera.

To move our camera, we rename our Main Camera to Camera for simplicity, and then add all the camera movement behavior in our game script that we will add to the main character Space Buddy.

Saving and loading

In this game, we would like to save and load data in our level, which in this case is the player's score, and we would like to load in a second level. All of this will be handled via a script.

Space Buddy the alien

We now add the main character in our game, which is the little alien named Space Buddy. To add the alien, we do the following:

1. Download the `alien.png` image from the following URL:

   `http://freeartsprites.com/platformer`

2. Move it to the sprites folder.

3. Create a sprite GameObject using the following image:

4. Name the GameObject `SpaceBuddy`.

5. Go to **Add Component | Physics 2D | Rigidbody 2D**.

6. Go to **Add Component | Physics 2D | Box Collider 2D**.

7. Go to **Add Component | New Script** and name the script `SpaceBuddy.js`.

8. In the Project Browser, add a folder named `Scripts` and move `SpaceBuddy.js` into it.

9. Add the following code to the script:

The first line of code is used to ensure strict typing — if you use the same variable for different data types, then an error will be thrown when building the script.

This prevents bugs related to incorrect data types from occurring. Have a look at the next line of code.

```
#pragma strict
```

Next, we define the vertical velocity of the character's jump as shown in the next line of code.

```
var power:float = 20.0;
```

Next, we define the speed or horizontal velocity that the character moves at when it moves towards the left-hand side or the right-hand side. Have a look at the next line of code.

```
var speed:float = 3.0;
```

In the next line of code, we define the vertical velocity that the camera travels at.

```
var camSpeed:float = 100.0;
```

In the next line of code, we set the vertical velocity that the lose trigger travels at.

```
var lavaSpeed:float = 100.0;
```

In the next code, we declare the main character as a Rigidbody.

```
var spacebuddy:Rigidbody2D;
```

 In the next line of code, we create a camera GameObject.

```
var cam:GameObject;
```

 In the next code, we declare the lose trigger GameObject.

```
var lava:GameObject;
```

 We declare a variable that will store the audio clip of the jump sound effect that we would like to play in the game.

```
var jumpclip:AudioClip;
```

 In the next code, we declare a variable that will store the audio clip of the win sound effect that we would like to play in the game.

```
var winclip: AudioClip;
```

 Then, in the next code, we declare a variable that will store the audio clip of the lose sound effect that we would like to play in the game.

```
var loseclip:AudioClip;
```

 We declare a variable to store the score in the game.

```
var score : float = 0.0;
```

We use the `Start` function when we want to enable a script before any of the `Update` functions are called. In this case, we want to use the conditional `if` statement to check that the current scene we are in is scene 2.

We use the Unity function `Application.LoadLevelName` to retrieve the name of the level that is currently loaded. We use the `==` operator to check that it matches with scene 2.

If there is no match, then it means that we are in scene 1 (the first level of the game) and, therefore, we do not need to play the success audio. However, when we do load the second scene, there will be a match, and thus, the success sound effect will play in the second level.

We call the audio now instead of at the end of level 1 because there is no time as the second level gets loaded instantly as soon as the first level has been passed. As is always the case, there are many ways of doing it, and another option would have been to add a delay before loading the next scene. Have a look at the next code.

```
function Start()
{
    if (Application.loadedLevelName == "scene2")
    {
```

To play the win sound effect, we use the `AudioSource.PlayClipAtPoint` Unity function. The first parameter that we pass is the `winclip` variable that holds the audio clip of the win sound effect, and then the second parameter we pass is the location from which the sound plays. Have a look at the next code.

```
AudioSource.PlayClipAtPoint(winclip, transform.position);
```

We only load our saved score from the previous level. If this is the first level, there will be no match in the preceding `if` statement and this script will not get called as we want to start the first level from 0. To load our score, we use the Unity function `PlayerPrefs.GetFloat` because our score is of the float data value. As the first parameter, we pass the same name that we used when we saved the data for that value, and then for the second parameter, we use the value that we set, should no pre-existing data be saved.

It is very important to assign this function to a variable as it returns the loaded value. Thus, we assign this to our `score` variable as we have loaded the saved score from the first level and want to carry it across to the next level. Have a look at the next code.

```
    score = PlayerPrefs.GetFloat("score",0);
  }
}
```

For this game, we would like to display the player's score. Using the existing Unity GUI function that gets called automatically, we create a rectangle with a size that we specify, consisting of the *x* and *y* coordinates denoting the starting position of the rectangle, followed by the *x* and *y* coordinates denoting the ending position.

We then add the string of text that we would like to display within the box followed by the + sign and the variable.

The + sign concatenates (joins) the variable into a string so that it can be displayed as a string as the GUI.Box method can only display string types. Have a look at the next code snippet.

```
function OnGUI()
{
  GUI.Box (Rect (10,10,100,30), "Score: "+score);
}
```

We call our MoveCharacter function within FixedUpdate instead of Update as we are using a Rigidbody — when using physics, we need to ensure that the updates occur in sync with the physics engine since using Update could cause inconsistencies depending on the frame rate of the game. Have a look at the next line of code.

```
function FixedUpdate()
{
  MoveCharacter();
}
```

In the next code snippet, we define a function to move the character.

```
function MoveCharacter()
{
```

In the next code, we detect if the input key from the keyboard is *A*.

```
    if (Input.GetKey(KeyCode.A))
    {
```

Move the character to the left-hand side using `transform.Translate`, which is the function that moves a GameObject's position based on direction and distance.

The first parameter passes the direction and the next two parameters, being speed and time, pass the distance since distance is speed over time. We use `vector3.left`, which is the shorthand for a predefined vector moving to the left-hand side, which is (-1,0,0).

We then multiply by the speed that we want the character to move to the left-hand side at, and then the amount of time we want the character to be moving to the left-hand side, which in this case is for as long as the player is pressing down the *A* key.

We use `Time.deltaTime` for this as it makes the movement frame-independent, allowing the character to move a certain distance per second instead of per frame because it calculates the seconds that have passed since the last frame. Have a look at the next line of code.

```
transform.Translate(Vector3.left * speed *
    Time.deltaTime);
}
```

In the next code, we detect if the input key from the keyboard is *D*.

```
if (Input.GetKey(KeyCode.D))
{
```

Move the character to the right-hand side using `transform.Translate`, which is the function that moves a GameObject's position based on direction and distance.

The first parameter passes the direction and the next two parameters, being the speed and time, pass the distance since distance is speed over time. We use `vector3.right`, which is the shorthand for a vector moving to the right-hand side.

We then multiply by the speed that we want the character to move to the right-hand side and by the amount of time we want the character to be moving to the right-hand side, which in this case is for as long as the player is pressing down the *D* key.

We use `Time.deltaTime` for this as it makes the movement frame-independent, allowing the character to move a certain distance per second instead of per frame because it calculates the seconds it took to complete the last frame. Have a look at the next code snippet.

```
        transform.Translate(Vector3.right * speed * Time.
deltaTime);
    }
}
```

In all our previous games, we made use of collision and the `OnCollisionEnter2D` function. However, this time, we are using a trigger instead, because we don't want the character to collide with the platforms, but instead pass through them; although, when the character passes through the platforms, we want the character to jump. Therefore, we use a trigger to check when the player is on a platform to trigger the jump, and thus we use the `OnTriggerEnter2D` function.

For the parameter of the function, we pass the collider of the GameObject that passes through the trigger to check which GameObject has collided with the trigger and therefore triggered it. Have a look at the next line of code.

```
function OnTriggerEnter2D (other:Collider2D)
{
```

We use the conditional `if` statement to check whether the GameObject `other`, that was passed through the function as a parameter, is a platform.

We check the name of the GameObject to check whether its name matches with the platform GameObject that is named `Platform`. Have a look at the next line of code

```
if(other.gameObject.name=="Platform")
{
```

The player increases their score by jumping. Each jump awards the player with 50 points. Therefore, since we know that Space Buddy has collided with the platform because the name of the collider matches, we assign our score variable the current score added with the 50 points.

We also play the jump sound effect on Space Buddy's collision with a platform. To play the jump sound effect, we use the `AudioSource.PlayClipAtPoint` Unity function.

The first parameter that we pass is the `jumpclip` variable that holds the audio clip of the jump sound effect, and then the second parameter we pass is the location from which the sound plays. Have a look at the next line of code.

```
score=score+50.0;
AudioSource.PlayClipAtPoint(jumpclip, transform.position);
```

 Each time that we award the player points to their score, we need to save the data, because if the game crashes or is interrupted, then we would lose the score. This way, we keep track of their progress. Also, we need to save the score to load it in the next level. Have a look at the next line of code.

```
PlayerPrefs.SetFloat("score", score);
```

 If the other GameObject's name is `Platform`, then that means that the character has collided with a platform and can jump on it. Thus, we move (accelerate) the character vertically in the *y* axis using a 2D vector.

We assign a new velocity to the character in the *y* axis by passing the `power` variable that we declared as the second parameter to the `vector2` function. Have a look at the next line of code.

```
spacebuddy.velocity = new Vector2(0,power);
```

 As the character is jumping up, it is only a matter of time until the character will jump off screen. Therefore, we need to find the camera in the scene and move it together with the character whenever the character jumps on a platform so that the character always remains in view.

To do this, we find the camera in the scene using the `Find` function and look for a match. Once the camera is found, we assign it to our `cam` variable to be used within our function. Have a look at the next line of code.

```
cam = GameObject.Find("Camera");
```

 When the character falls to the bottom, hits the lava, and dies, it is game over. Thus, we have a trigger that we name `lava` below the camera to check that they have fallen and hit the lava. We use the `Find` function to find the `lava` trigger within the scene. Have a look at the next line of code.

```
lava = GameObject.Find("Lava");
```

 We move the camera up together with the character whenever the character jumps on a platform so that the character always remains onscreen. Have a look at the next line of code.

```
cam.transform.Translate(Vector3.up * camSpeed *
   Time.deltaTime);
```

We move the lava trigger up whenever the character jumps on a platform and the camera moves up.

If we didn't move the lava trigger up, and if a character fell below the camera, there is a chance that the character may land on a platform and not reach the lava trigger's initial position, therefore never ending the game.

Thus, we raise the lava trigger up together with the character and camera on a platform jump so that it is always in the correct location (just below the camera and above any platforms) and cannot be missed. It also adds to the immersion having the lava rise up. Have a look at the next line of code.

```
lava.transform.Translate(Vector3.up * lavaSpeed *
   Time.deltaTime);
}
```

We use the conditional `if` statement to check whether the GameObject `other`, that was passed through the function as a parameter, is the lava trigger. We check the name of the GameObject to check whether its name matches with the lava GameObject that is named `Lava`. Have a look at the next line of code.

```
if(other.gameObject.name=="Lava")
{
```

If the `other` GameObject's name is `Lava`, then that means that the character has collided with the lava trigger and thus triggered it. To play the sound effect for losing, we use the `AudioSource.PlayClipAtPoint` Unity function. The first parameter that we pass is the `loseclip` variable that holds the audio clip of the lose sound effect, and then the second parameter we pass is the location from which the sound plays.

Triggering the lava trigger means that we can stop the game since it is game over. To stop the game, we use `Time.timescale` as it sets the amount of time at which time is passing. Setting it to 0 slows it to a stop. Have a look at the next code.

```
AudioSource.PlayClipAtPoint(loseclip,
   transform.position);
      Time.timeScale = 0;
}
```

To successfully complete a level, the player must get Space Buddy safely into the UFO beam at the very top of the level.

We use the conditional `if` statement to check whether the GameObject `other`, that was passed through the function as a parameter, is the `UFObeam` trigger.

We check the name of the GameObject to check whether its name matches with the `UFObeam` GameObject that is named `UFObeam`. Have a look at the next line of code.

```
if(other.gameObject.name=="UFObeam")
{
```

If the `other` GameObject's name is `UFObeam` instead of `Lava`, then that means that the character has collided with the `UFObeam` trigger, and thus triggered it.

Triggering the `UFObeam` trigger means that the player has completed level 1 successfully, and we can therefore load level 2. To load level 2, we use the Unity function `Application.LoadLevel` and pass the name of the level that we want to load as its parameter. We then check the name of the GameObject to check whether its name matches with the `UFObeam2` GameObject that is named `UFObeam2`.

```
Application.LoadLevel("Scene2");
}

if(other.gameObject.name=="UFObeam2")
{
```

Triggering the `UFObeam2` trigger (which we will make later on in the chapter) means we can play the winning sound effect and stop the game since the game has been completed successfully. To play the win sound effect, we use the `AudioSource.PlayClipAtPoint` Unity function.

The first parameter that we pass is the `winclip` variable that holds the audio clip of the win sound effect, and then the second parameter we pass is the location from which the sound plays.

To stop the game, we use `Time.timescale` as it sets the amount of time at which time is passing. Setting it to `0` slows it to a stop. Have a look at the next line of code.

```
AudioSource.PlayClipAtPoint(winclip,
    transform.position);
Time.timeScale = 0;
    }
}
```

We can now build the script.

Space Buddy script

The following screenshot shows all the variables that we created in our script:

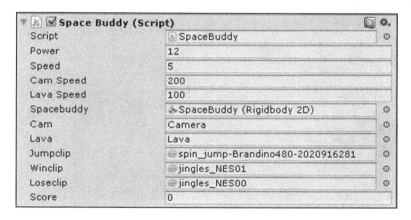

We may need to adjust (decrease) the power field for our level. The higher the power, the higher the character's jump! Try changing the power until it suits your needs. Do not be afraid of experimenting since game creation takes a fair amount of iteration to ensure that we get exactly what we are looking for.

We need to make sure that none of the fields are empty and there is no missing data.

In the Inspector, our Space Buddy script needs to match the preceding screenshot, and thus if the assets are not already assigned to the correct GameObject, we need to assign them so that they can be used in the script.

We need to assign assets to the following variables:

- Spacebuddy Rigidbody 2D — to control our character
- Camera — so that we can move it
- Lava — so that we can raise it
- Audio clips — to play them

Positioning

We position the first scene's game objects to match the following screenshot:

The second scene

To learn and practice using multiple levels, we will add a second scene. For the second scene, let's execute the following steps:

1. Create a new scene and save it as Scene2.

2. We move this scene into the Scenes folder in the Project Browser.

3. We repeat all the preceding steps except that we use the alternative second scene sprites.

4. We name all the objects the exact same names as in the first scene except for the UFObeam GameObject, which we name UFObeam2 because it has unique code associated with it.

5. We position the second scene's GameObjects to match the following screenshot:

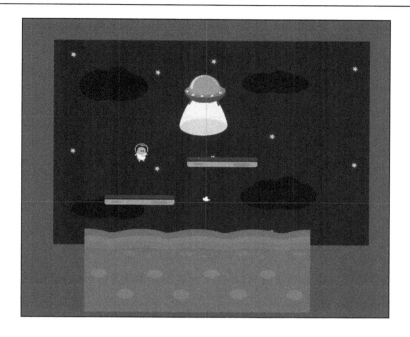

The final result

The final layout for the Project Browser should look like the following screenshot:

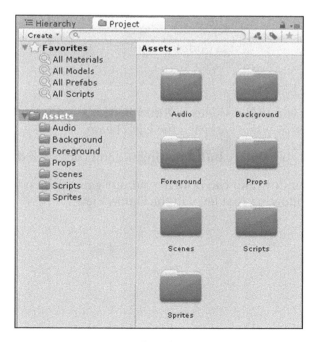

The final hierarchy for the first scene should look like the following screenshot:

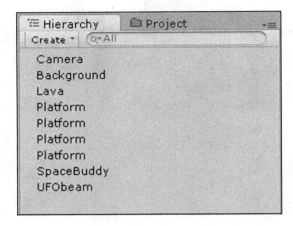

The final hierarchy for the second scene should look like the following screenshot:

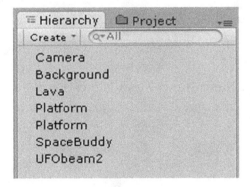

We must remember to add the scenes to **Build Settings** – at least the second one, or it will throw an error when we reach the UFO beam.

To do this, we must go to **File | Build Settings...** and click on **Add Current**.

We then close the window and can now try out our game. When we push play, we should see the following first level in the Game View:

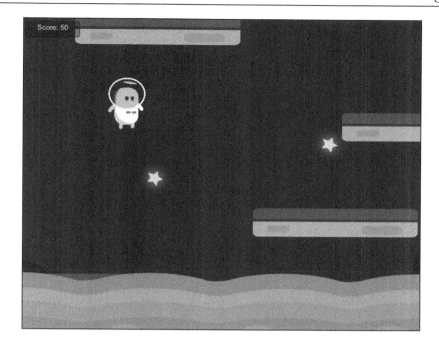

We should then see the following second level in the Game View once we have successfully completed the first level:

Deployment

It is an amazing feeling to create your very own game, although releasing and sharing a game to be enjoyed by others can be even more exhilarating. Having others experience your world and enjoy it is very rewarding.

We will learn how to deploy our games so that we can run them on different platforms and share them with our family, friends, and the public.

Also, while developing our game, we need to test the game we are creating on its target platform so that we can test its unique platform-specific features.

To deploy our game, we do the following:

1. Go to **File | Build Settings...**.

2. Make sure you are in the first scene by clicking on the scene twice in the Project Browser, and then add the current scene in **Build Settings**.

3. Now, make sure you are in the second scene by clicking on **Scene2** twice in the Project Browser, and then add the current scene in **Build Settings**. Make sure that they are both ticked.

4. Select your target platform (in this case, PC). Select whether or not it is for 32-bit or 64-bit and whether it is a release build or development build.

5. A development build is usually slower than the release build and contains extra features to debug.

6. The **Player Settings...** button has extra settings, whereby we can add our own icon and splash an image for our game.

7. We simply click on the **Build** button, save our game to the location of choice, and give our game a name (in this case, Space Buddy).

8. We now have our very own PC game executable (the .exe file).

9. When we open it, we can select its settings and even edit the game controls, giving even greater flexibility.

10. Follow the same steps for all other platforms; however, each will have its own extra requirements. For instance, for iOS deployment, you will require a Mac with Xcode, and for Android mobile devices, you will require the Android SDK.

11. Had we chosen Web Player, we would receive an HTML file that we could double-click to play within our browser offline. We can then host it on a website for others to enjoy online.

The following screenshot displays the **Build Settings** screen:

Your journey ahead

Now that we have learned the essential building blocks of 2D game development, we are ready to create our very own games. The only way to truly learn is to keep practicing. We need to start simple, create what we are passionate about, and then as we become better and more confident, we can try out new things and increase the complexity.

We should not let failure set us back, but instead learn from our mistakes. Perseverance is the key.

There is always more than one way to do something, and through consistent practice and research, we will discover which method is better suited to our needs. Games are constantly evolving, and as such, there is always more to discover. We have merely scratched the surface and have an incredible journey ahead!

A plethora of resources

As Unity is such a prominent game engine, there is a huge wealth of information and resources available at our disposal.

Online resources

The following is a list of online resources:

- `http://www.google.com`: The first and foremost location to search for information should be on the biggest and most popular search engine.

- `http://www.unity3d.com`: The next essential location for Unity-related information is the official Unity site.

- `http://unity3d.com/learn`: If you are looking to learn more, then this learn section provides all methods of learning.

- `http://unity3d.com/unity/whats-new`: To keep up to date with the latest Unity releases and bug fixes, this is a good resource.

- `https://store.unity3d.com`: To upgrade your version of Unity, should you require the extra features (enabling you to compare the different versions).

- `http://forum.unity3d.com`: There is a huge, helpful Unity community of experienced developers. Learn from the best by corresponding and collaborating with them on the Unity forums. It also provides networking opportunities.

- `http://answers.unity3d.com`: For Unity support, the answers section is invaluable in providing clear answers. You can usually find that a question you may have has already been asked and answered.

- `http://learnunity2d.com`: This is a great site that pulls together all 2D Unity related tutorials, videos, and games.

- `http://thegamesvine.com`: This is a new and awesome site for all things game related, learning about game development, game news, reviews, and purchasing games at bargain deals.

- `http://gamesdesigner.net`: This is my portfolio website.

Offline events

Unite Conference — an annual Unity developer's conference, whereby the Unity community get together. You can meet the Unity developers as well as find out about their roadmap ahead. Live practical training in much greater depth is also provided. You can find these at the following URL:

`https://unity3d.com/unite`

There are other Unity workshops, user groups, and events that take place in different countries and cities. If there is none available in your area, then why not start your very own.

Free resources

Remember to always get the rights and permissions in writing to use resources, whether publicly available or not, and to check that there is no infringement of trademarked, patented, or copyrighted work.

Simply referencing or citing a work does not constitute fair use.

The following is a list of sites that offer free resources:

- `http://freeartsprites.com`: If you are looking for a website that you do not need to cite and has public-domain, royalty-free sprites to use in your very own commercial or non-commercial games, then this is an ideal place. If you wish for sprites that can be used without any worries, then I urge you to go to the following site that we have used throughout the book.

- `http://opengameart.org`: This is another site that contains public-domain art that can be used freely; however, use it with caution since it combines free art with art that has many other restrictions, so always check what the conditions are.

- `http://www.blender.org`: Blender is freely available, open source 3D modeling software that can be used for both commercial and non-commercial purposes.

- `http://www.getpaint.net`: Paint.Net is a free 2D graphics creation and editing software that can be used for any purpose.

- `http://www.gimp.org`: Gimp is another alternative to Paint.NET.

- `http://audacity.sourceforge.net`: Audacity is a free, open source, cross-platform audio recording and editing software.

Hosting games

This is an incredible indie website that I really like. If you would like to easily make your PC game available to the public—whether for free or paid—then I recommend the following website as it also has the extra option to allow people to decide if they would like to donate to your game:

```
http://itch.io
```

Social media

If you would like to catch up with me on Twitter, my Twitter username is as follows:

```
@Atinev
```

Summary

In this final chapter, we learned about audio, feedback, and deploying our game. We have put everything that we have learned throughout the book into creating a game similar to Doodle Jump. We were then guided on our onward journey in 2D game development with a selection of useful resources.

Index

Symbols

2D project
  creating 9, 10

A

Accelerate function 138
acceleration 186
accelerometer 107
acid sprite
  URL, for downloading 156
agile ninja character, endless runner
  animator parameters, adding 170
  animator states, setting 170-172
  creating 167
  jump animation, creating 168, 169
  movement controls, setting 172-175
  run animation, creating 167, 168
  slide animation, creating 169
  transitions, ordering 170-172
alien.png image
  URL, for downloading 217
alien, Space Buddy
  adding 217-226
  positioning 228
  script, building 227
ambient sound effects 208
angular drag 187
animation clip
  creating, in Dopesheet 70, 71
Animation Editor
  used, for animating sprite 70
Animation 23

Animator
  about 24, 72, 73
  used, for controlling Roguelike hero
    movement 128, 129
Application Programming Interfaces
  (APIs) 88
assembly language
  about 77
  code representation 77
assets, Project Browser
  creating 15
  searching 16
Asset Store. *See* **Unity Asset Store**
Audacity
  URL 235
audio
  about 108
  adding 208
  adding, to Space Buddy 215, 216
  music 208
  sound effects 208
automatic slicing, sprite sheet
  about 56, 57
  with Grid option 57, 59

B

background 27
background asset
  assigning, to GameObject 34
  alternative method, for assigning
    to GameObject 38, 39
  importing 28, 29
  toolbar method, for assigning to
    GameObject 35, 36

background, setting with static image
  about 28
  background asset, assigning to
    GameObject 34
  background asset, importing 28, 29
  GameObject, setting 39
  sprite settings 30
background, setting with tileset
  about 28, 40
  corner pieces, using 41
  grid settings 41
  prefab, creating 41
  seamless textures, using 41
basic quantities, physics
  acceleration 186
  angular drag 187
  collision 187
  damping 187
  drag 187
  force 186
  friction 187
  gravity 187
  inertia 187
  length 186
  mass 186
  matter 186
  momentum 187
  rigid body 186
  space 186
  time 186
  vectors 186
  velocity 186
binary code. *See* **machine language**
binary digits (bits) 76
Blender
  URL 235
Boo code
  versus C# code 79, 80
  versus UnityScript code 79, 80
boolean data type 82
Boulder.png image
  URL, for downloading 175
Box2D 189-191
buttons
  about 112
  creating 112

  creating, GUILayout.Button function
    used 112, 113
  creating, OnGUI function used 112

C

camera
  about 107
  adding, to Space Buddy 216
  using 210
cannonballs, physics game
  creating 202, 203
cannon, physics game
  creating 197-202
C# code
  versus Boo code 79, 80
  versus UnityScript code 79, 80
character, hello world program
  adding 63-66
  controlling 92, 93
class
  about 87
  accessibility level 88
  scope level 88
classic arcade
  bathroom environment, creating 148, 149
  conditions 158
  creating 147
  font style, editing 160, 161
  game controls, adding 150-152
  HUD, adding 159
  spawning acid, adding 156, 157
  spawning grime, adding 153-156
  Spongy 148
  Spongy, adding 149, 150
  testing 163
ClassicArcade.zip
  URL, for downloading 149
code
  components 81
  need for 76
code editor 89
colliders 190
collision 187
Collision Detection
  settings 193

comments
  using 87
components, code
  classes 87
  comments 87
  conditional statement 86
  data types 81, 82
  functions 83-86
  operators 82, 83
components, Physics 2D
  colliders 190
  joints 190
  rigidbodies 190
computer programmer 75
conditional statement
  about 86
  if...else 86
conditions, classic arcade
  lives, adding 158
  score, adding 158, 159
  time, adding 158, 159
Console View 22
controller vibration 109
coroutines 99

D

damping 187
data
  loading 209
  saving 209
data types
  about 81
  boolean 82
  float 82
  GameObject 82
  integer 82
  string 82
Debug.Log() function 112
desert_BG.png image
  URL, for downloading 179
Dopesheet
  about 70
  animation clip, creating 70, 71
drag 187
draw call batching 61

DwarfSpriteSheet file
  URL, for downloading 136

E

endless runner
  about 165
  advantage 166
  agile ninja character, creating 166
  creating, parallax scrolling used 178-180
  expanding 183
  obstacles, creating 175-177
  overview 165, 166
  particle effects, creating 180
  survival 178
  testing 183
  timer, displaying 181, 182
enemy, hello world program
  destroying, steps 94-98
enemy, Roguelike
  animating 138
  movement, scripting 138, 139
  spawning 136, 137
environment, physics game
  background, creating 194, 195
  foreground, creating 195, 196
  scene, creating 194
external libraries
  importing 88
extra Views
  about 22
  Animation 23
  Animator 24
  Console 22
  Profiler 24
  Sprite Editor 23

F

feedback sound effects 208
file formats, sprite 49, 50
Filter Mode, sprite settings
  Bilinear 32
  Point 32
  Trilinear 32
Find() method 139
float data type 82

font style
  editing 160, 161
force 186
foreground
  setting 43
Format, Platform Settings
  16 bits 33
  Compressed 33
  Truecolor 33
frames per second (FPS) 71
free resources, Unity 235
friction 187
function
  about 83
  calling 84
  declaring 84
  multiple variables, passing to 85
  variable, passing to 84
  variable, returning from 85

G

galaxy.png image
  URL, for downloading 212
game controller 106
game controls
  about 114
  raycasting 114-117
game development's background 7, 8
GameObject
  about 82
  background asset, assigning to 34
  background color, setting 39
  background layer, setting 39
  background position, setting 39
  creating 19
Game View, Unity Editor interface 14
garbage collection 161
Gimp
  URL 235
GPS 107
Graphical User Interface (GUI) 108
graphic design software. See image
    editing software
Grassbg.png image
  URL 122
gravity 187

grime sprite
  URL, for downloading 153
GUI.box function 182, 199
GUILayout.Button function
  used, for creating buttons 112, 113
GUI sound effects 208
gyroscope 107

H

heads-up display. See HUD
hello world program
  creating 90, 91
hero, Roguelike
  animating 123
  movement, controlling 128
  Walking Down animation 124-126
  Walking Left animation 126
  Walking Right animation 127
  Walking Up animation 127
Hierarchy tab, Unity Editor interface
  about 18
  GameObjects, creating 19
  parenting 18
High Dynamic Range (HDR) 43
high-level languages
  about 77
  code representation 78
HUD
  about 108, 159
  adding 159

I

if...else conditional statement 86
image editing software
  used, for creating sprite 46, 47
inertia 187
input
  about 103
  detecting 111
  in games 104
  types 106, 107
  versus output 103
Input.GetAxis() function 111
Input.GetButton() function 111
Input Manager

about 110
advantages 110
configuring 110, 111
input, types
accelerometer 107
camera 107
game controller 106
GPS 107
gyroscope 107
joystick 107
keyboard 106
microphone 107
motion controller 107
mouse 106
stylus 107
touchscreen 107
Inspector
about 20
components, adding 21
components, removing 21
Instantiate() function 201
integer data type 82
interpolate 187
Interpolate settings
options 192
InvokeRepeating function 138

J

jingles_NES00.ogg
URL, for downloading 216
jingles_NES01.ogg
URL, for downloading 216
joints 190
joystick 107

K

keyboard 106
kinematic 187

L

lava.png image
URL, for downloading 214
length 186
levels, programming languages
about 79

assembly language 77
high-level languages 77
machine language 76
lossless image compression 49

M

machine language
about 76, 77
visual representation 77
Main Camera option
Background parameter 42
Clear Flags parameter 42
Clipping Planes parameter 43
Culling Mask parameter 42
Depth parameter 43
HDR parameter 43
Occlusion Cullling parameter 43
Projection parameter 43
Rendering Path parameter 43
Size parameter 43
Target Texture parameter 43
Viewport Rect parameter 43
manual slicing, sprite sheet
selection area, adding 54, 55
selection area, removing 54, 55
Toolbar controls 55
mass 186
matter 186
microphone 107
mipmaps 32
momentum 187
MonoDevelop
about 89
opening 89, 90
motion controller 107
mouse 106
movement controls
setting, for agile ninja character of endless
runner 172-175
movement, Roguelike enemy
scripting 138, 139
movement, Roguelike hero
controlling, with Animator
component 128, 129
scripting 130-135
multiplayer

adding 210, 211
pass and play 211
real time 211
multiple variables
passing, to function 85
music 208

N

namespaces 100
NinjaSpriteSheet.png image
URL, for downloading 167
Notepad 89

O

obstacles, endless runner
creating 175-177
offline events, Unity 235
OnGUI function
about 144
used, for creating buttons 112
online resources, Unity 234
operators
about 82
arithmetic operators 83
logical operators 83
relational operators 83
Orb.png sprite
URL, for downloading 141
output
in games 105
types 107
versus input 103
output, types
audio 108
controller vibration 109
visual output 108

P

Packing Tag, sprite settings 31
Paint.NET
about 47
URL, for downloading 47, 235
parallax scrolling
used, for creating endless runner 178-180
parenting 18

particle effects
creating, for endless runner 180
pass and play 211
Photoshop 47
physical quantities, physics
interpolate 187
kinematic 187
static 187
physics
about 186
basic quantities 186
physical quantities 187
Physics 2D
about 187
accessing 188
Box2D 189
components 190
Physics 2D Manager settings
Default Material 188
Gravity 188
Layer Collision Matrix 189
Position Iterations 188
Raycast Hit Trigger 188
Velocity Iterations 188
Physics 2D Material
about 189
creating 189
physics game
cannonballs, creating 202, 203
cannon, creating 197-202
creating 194
environment, creating 194
extending 205
final result 203, 204
Pivot, sprite settings 32
Pixels to Units, sprite settings 31
platform.png image
URL, for downloading 213
Platform Settings, sprite
Format 33
Max Size 33
prefab 41
private functions 88
Profiler 24
programming languages
about 76
levels 76-79

Project Browser
  about 15
  assets, creating 15, 16
  assets, importing 17
  assets, searching 16
  favorites, setting 16
  final layout 203
props, physics game
  adding 196
  crate, adding 196
  plank, adding 197
public domain art
  URL, for downloading 114
public functions 88

R

raster image
  versus vector image 48
raycasting 114-117
real time 211
resource management 161-163
resulting environment
  foreground, setting 43
  Main Camera option 42
  setting 41
rigidbodies
  about 190
  creating 191-193
rigid body 186
Rigidbody 2D
  settings 192
Roguelike
  about 120
  advantages 120
  background, adding 122
  collisions, detecting 143
  creating, Unity used 119
  enemy, animating 138
  enemy, spawning 136, 137
  hero, animating 123
  permadeath 144
  shooting projectiles, adding 141-143

S

Scene View, Unity Editor interface 14
scripting languages 78

second scene, Space Buddy
  adding 228
Sleeping Mode
  settings 192
Software Development Kits (SDKs) 88
sound effects
  about 208
  ambient sound effects 208
  feedback sound effects 208
  GUI sound effects 208
space 186
Space Buddy
  alien, adding 217
  audio, adding 215, 216
  camera, adding 216
  creating 211
  data, loading 217
  data, saving 217
  deploying 232
  extending 233, 234
  final result 229-231
  first scene, creating 212
  galaxy, creating 212
  lava, creating 214
  platform, adding 213
  second scene, adding 228
  triggers, adding 213
  UFO beam, creating 215
spin_jump.wav
  URL, for downloading 215
sprite
  about 46
  animating 69
  animating, Animation Editor used 70
  creating 46
  creating, image editing software
    used 46, 47
  file formats 49, 50
  importing, into Unity 50
  raster image, versus vector image 48
  sprite sheet 47
Sprite Editor
  about 23
  used, for slicing sprite sheet 52
sprite image
  URL 49
Sprite Mode, sprite settings 31

sprite packer 62, 63
Sprite Renderer
about 66-68
Color field 68
Material field 68
Order in Layer option 68
Sorting Layer option 68
Sprite field 67
sprite settings
applying 34
Filter Mode 30, 32
Packing Tag 31
Pivot 32
Pixels to Units 31
Platform Settings 30, 33
Sprite Mode 30, 31
Texture Type 30, 31
sprite sheet
about 47
automatic slicing 56, 57
manual slicing 53, 54
slicing 51
slicing, Sprite Editor used 52
Start() function 84, 139
static 187
static image
used, for setting background 28
string data type 82
stylus 107

T

tags
creating 161
texture atlas 61
texture atlasing
about 31, 61
sprite packer 62, 63
Texture Type, sprite settings 30, 31
tileset
about 40
used, for setting background 28
time 186
timer, endless runner
displaying 181, 182
Toolbar, Unity Editor interface 12
touchscreen 107

Transform Gizmo toggles
about 13
Layers drop-down box 13
Layout drop-down menu 13
Transform tools, Unity Editor interface
about 12
Rotate 12
Scale 12
Translate 12
trigger
creating 209
Typing 81

U

UFObeam.png image
URL, for downloading 215
Unity
about 8
downloading 8
free resources 235
games, hosting 236
installing 8
offline events 235
online resources 234
setting up 8, 9
sprite, importing into 50
URL 8
used, for creating Roguelike 119
Unity Asset Store 17
Unity Editor interface
about 11
Game View 14
Hierarchy tab 18
Inspector 20
Project Browser 15
Scene View 14
Toolbar 12
Transform tools 12
Views 11
UnityScript 78
UnityScript code
versus Boo code 79, 80
versus C# code 79, 80
Unity Scripting Reference
about 100-102
URL, for accessing 101
Update() method 84, 139

V

variable
  passing, to function 84
  returning, from function 85
vector image
  versus raster image 48
vectors 186
velocity 186
visual output 108

W

WizardSpriteSheet.png
  URL 123

X

Xara 47

Thank you for buying
Learning Unity 2D Game Development by Example

About Packt Publishing

Packt, pronounced 'packed', published its first book "*Mastering phpMyAdmin for Effective MySQL Management*" in April 2004 and subsequently continued to specialize in publishing highly focused books on specific technologies and solutions.

Our books and publications share the experiences of your fellow IT professionals in adapting and customizing today's systems, applications, and frameworks. Our solution based books give you the knowledge and power to customize the software and technologies you're using to get the job done. Packt books are more specific and less general than the IT books you have seen in the past. Our unique business model allows us to bring you more focused information, giving you more of what you need to know, and less of what you don't.

Packt is a modern, yet unique publishing company, which focuses on producing quality, cutting-edge books for communities of developers, administrators, and newbies alike. For more information, please visit our website: www.packtpub.com.

Writing for Packt

We welcome all inquiries from people who are interested in authoring. Book proposals should be sent to author@packtpub.com. If your book idea is still at an early stage and you would like to discuss it first before writing a formal book proposal, contact us; one of our commissioning editors will get in touch with you.

We're not just looking for published authors; if you have strong technical skills but no writing experience, our experienced editors can help you develop a writing career, or simply get some additional reward for your expertise.

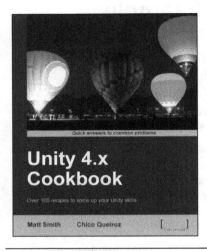

Unity 4.x Cookbook

ISBN: 978-1-84969-042-3   Paperback: 386 pages

Over 100 recipes to spice up your Unity skills

1. A wide range of topics are covered, ranging in complexity, offering something for every Unity 4 game developer.

2. Every recipe provides step-by-step instructions, followed by an explanation of how it all works, and alternative approaches or refinements.

3. Book developed with the latest version of Unity (4.x).

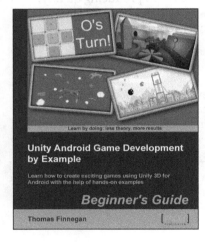

Unity Android Game Development by Example Beginner's Guide

ISBN: 978-1-84969-201-4   Paperback: 320 pages

Learn how to create exciting games using Unity 3D for Android with the help of hands-on examples

1. Enter the increasingly popular mobile market and create games using Unity 3D and Android.

2. Learn optimization techniques for efficient mobile games.

3. Clear, step-by-step instructions for creating a complete mobile game experience.

Please check **www.PacktPub.com** for information on our titles

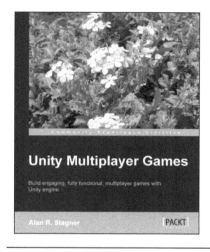

Unity Multiplayer Games

ISBN: 978-1-84969-232-8   Paperback: 242 pages

Build engaging, fully functional, multiplayer games with Unity engine

1.   Create a variety of multiplayer games and apps in the Unity 4 game engine, still maintaining compatibility with Unity 3.

2.   Employ the most popular networking middleware options for Unity games.

3.   Packed with ideas, inspiration, and advice for your own game design and development.

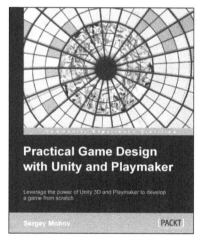

Practical Game Design with Unity and Playmaker

ISBN: 978-1-84969-810-8   Paperback: 122 pages

Leverage the power of Unity 3D and Playmaker to develop a game from scratch

1.   Create artificial intelligence for a game using Playmaker.

2.   Learn how to integrate a game with external APIs (Kongregate).

3.   Learn how to quickly develop games in Unity and Playmaker.

4.   A step-by-step game development tutorial using AI scripting, external APIs, and Multiplayer implementation.

Please check **www.PacktPub.com** for information on our titles

www.ingramcontent.com/pod-product-compliance
Lightning Source LLC
Chambersburg PA
CBHW060534060326
40690CB00017B/3489